# VENABLES' ENGLAND

Also by Terry Venables

*THEY USED TO PLAY ON GRASS*
(with Gordon Williams)

*HAZELL PLAYS SOLOMON*
(with Gordon Williams)

*HAZELL AND THE THREE-CARD TRICK*
(with Gordon Williams)

*HAZELL AND THE MENACING JESTER*
(with Gordon Williams)

*VENABLES*
*The Autobiography*
(with Neil Hanson)

Also by Jane Nottage

*PAUL GASCOIGNE*
*The Inside Story*

*THE ITALIANS*

*THE ITALIAN FOOTBALL DIET AND*
*FITNESS PROGRAMME*

# VENABLES' ENGLAND

## THE MAKING OF THE TEAM

Terry Venables
with Jane Nottage

B🍃XTREE

First published in Great Britain in 1996 by Boxtree Limited,
Broadwall House, 21 Broadwall, London SE1 9PL

Copyright © Terence Venables Limited 1996

The right of Terence Venables Limited to be identified as Author of
this work has been asserted by it in accordance with the Copyright,
Designs and Patents Act 1988

1 3 5 7 9 10 8 6 4 2

ISBN 0 7522 1664 3

Typeset by SX Composing DTP, Rayleigh, Essex
Plate section designed by Roger Lightfoot
Graphics by Slatter-Anderson
Printed and bound in Great Britain by Bath Press

A CIP catalogue entry for this book is available
from the British Library

# CONTENTS

# FOREWORD

## BY YVETTE VENABLES

I could certainly never have imagined what the future would bring when Terry and I first set eyes on each other, but to this day I wouldn't have changed anything. We have been blissfully happy together for many years and I hope we will spend the rest of our lives together. Terry has more than fulfilled all my romantic aspirations of what the man of my dreams would be like. He is my best friend and confidant as well as my husband, and I don't think any woman could ask for more than that. He is also honest, kind and thoughtful, and we both share a good sense of humour. It's really important to be able to laugh, even when things get you down.

I think that one of the reasons why we have such a successful relationship is because we have faced all the ups and downs of life together and have always been in total agreement as to how to handle certain situations, like the battle with Alan Sugar. There was never any doubt in my mind that Terry should fight to clear his name. I was angry and shocked that someone could be so vicious and unfair. There was never any question of us giving up the fight because of pressure. We are both determined to see it through to the bitter end. I feel it is only right that Terry should be allowed to fight back and claim what is rightfully his.

Some time after Terry and I met we went to Barcelona. We had a great time: he used to go to the club in the mornings, and then we would meet up for lunch and a swim and have a siesta before dinner. You eat really late in Spain, so we would be out until four or five in the morning. I have never been that interested in football, but I used to go to the matches in Barcelona, as it was more of a family affair. All the wives, girlfriends and children would turn up and enjoy an afternoon's entertainment. We used to have a good chat as well as watching the action.

I don't think it is the same in England. In fact, when Terry moved to Tottenham, I stopped going as I didn't really feel comfortable sitting alone or going into the directors' box. Terry used to worry about me at the matches and so we both decided it was best if I didn't attend them. As Terry said: 'Men don't usually take their wives to work with them, so you don't have to come and watch me working.' But I still remained very close to his professional life and I would share the joy of winning and the sorrow of losing.

Terry and I have never been big on socializing. We enjoy going out with a small group of close friends, but we both dislike going to big parties. Terry is a bit better than me about this because he has to be, but basically our idea of a good, relaxing evening is for the two of us to either eat at our club Scribes West in Kensington, or west London, or go to a nearby restaurant in Knightsbridge called Montpeliano. Then we'll go home and watch television together. As I've said, he's my best friend and I'm his, and we are getting more and more self-contained. He's the centre of my life and I find that I don't want to see other people, which is not altogether a good idea because it can isolate you from your friends. But I suppose after everything we went through together during the last two and a half years, we have bound together into an even stronger unit and there is less room for the people we meet through business.

I particularly dislike going to big functions. I never feel comfortable and dislike the fact that when we arrive everyone is saying, 'Oh look, there's the England Coach,' and then looking at me to see what his wife is like.

However, I have to be on show nearly every day as I have become the manager of Scribes. This was more by default than design. The last manager left, so I was asked if I could take over. It was quite a challenge as I hadn't had any previous experience, but over the last few years I have learnt how to run the club and we are doing quite well, though I have to admit that I am someone who really enjoys working around the home, rather than within the confines of an office.

When I was at home people used to say, 'Don't you get bored?', but I can honestly say I was never bored when I was at home. I'm self-motivated and I enjoy doing all the things that people say they will do if they don't have to work. I used to have piano lessons, go to pottery classes, organize the garden, do some creative painting and decorate the house, and also go to the gym three times a week. In spite of what some people think, you don't have to vegetate at home – it is just an attitude of mind.

While Terry is watching a match on a Saturday afternoon, I always go and see my mum. My brother, his wife and their three children come over as well and we all meet up. Apart from visits to my family, I spent a lot of time at home addicted to the O. J. Simpson trial. I used to sit up late watching it. In the end I got quite good at predicting the moves the various lawyers would make, so I am thinking of using it as my specialist subject on *Mastermind!* After I had watched the trial, we were watching a programme on football journalists. One of the questions put was 'How do you have the right to criticize the top footballing people? Where do you get your knowledge from?' and the reply was 'Well, when you start, you go to football matches, talk to players and managers and that gives you the ability to write about what they are doing.' I think it is bizarre that journalists can write about and be critical of the way you have played a game, which players you have chosen etc., without any real knowledge. It is also annoying that some of them think they have as much knowledge as Terry or people in his position. Does that mean that after watching O. J. Simpson's trial every day for nine months, you know as much as a barrister?

Obviously, after all these years together, Terry and I have got to know each other pretty well. Quite a lot of people have asked me if he has any irritating habits, and, apart from scribbling tactics all over the place, he hasn't. I often come down to breakfast in the morning to find tactics all over John Major's head on the front of the *Daily Mail!* He also has the usual male habit of hanging his jackets on the banister rails and then wondering why there are humps imprinted on the back!

I, on the other hand, have a very irritating habit of making noises in my sleep. I talk, laugh, cry and impersonate things, which can lead to some funny moments in our lives. Terry has often got up in the middle of the night because he thinks there is a bird stuck in the room, and then discovered it's me whistling in my sleep. The funniest incident happened when I heard a helicopter over-head in the middle of the night. I woke Terry and we decided the police must be looking for some escaped convict. Anyway, it disap-peared after a few minutes and we went back to sleep, until Terry suddenly woke me to say he'd heard footsteps on the cobblestones outside our house. We were convinced it must be the person the helicopter was looking for, so armed with the rod we use to open our skylight windows, Terry crept down the stairs followed by me, hobbling – at the time I had my leg in plaster as I was recovering from a knee operation. He opened the front door and leapt into the bushes brandishing the rod, but no one was there. He had a good look around but there was nobody in sight.

Eventually we returned to bed and fell asleep. The next morn-ing. Terry rang me from the car and said, 'Did that strange noise sound like this?' He then made a clucking sound. And of course it dawned on me that it had been me making sounds in my sleep again.

But back to the England job. I was very pleased when it was first suggested that Terry was the man for the job. I thought it would be great for him personally and also that it would vindicate him in the face of the awful allegations he had been subjected to over the past year or so. It would mean that the man in the street would stop and think, 'Hang on a minute, he can't have done all those awful things if the FA are willing to put him in charge of their national football team.'

The only hesitation I had in him accepting the job was in con-nection with the media. Bearing in mind what Graham Taylor and Bobby Robson had been through, I thought our lives would be made a nightmare by the press. But having said that, nothing could be worse than being slaughtered in the press on a daily basis for months on end, which we'd experienced when Terry left Tottenham and decided to fight for his right to have his contract honoured.

In the end I came to the conclusion that it was one of those jobs that if it was offered to you, you simply couldn't refuse it. When things really hotted up and it looked certain that Terry was going to get it, we did sit down together and discuss turning it down and going abroad, but we decided it was something that you just had to do or you'd always regret it. You'd go through the rest of your life wondering what would have happened if you'd taken it.

The experience with Tottenham has definitely changed Terry. It may seem naïve, but he used to trust everyone – when you are honest yourself then you expect other people to think in the same way – but he's found that not everyone is honest, and so he is a bit more wary of people's motives. Some of the things people do to each other are unbelievable. We've lived through the whole spectrum of good and bad.

Terry is basically a forgiving person, but I'm afraid I find it difficult to be pleasant to people who disappeared when the going got tough. I find it frustrating that he can be nice to people who have done or said horrible things about us.

The possibility of the England job seemed to drag on endlessly, with daily speculation in the press, but just when we thought that no one would ever come to a final decision, it was suddenly all decided. It was Tuesday 25 January 1994 and I'd gone to my piano lesson and done some shopping. I was at home cleaning the kitchen floor when at five-thirty in the afternoon the phone rang. It was Terry. 'Where are you?' I asked him. 'I'm in a hotel and I've just come out of the meeting,' he replied. 'How's it going?' I asked. 'It's done – I'm the new England Coach.'

I could tell by his voice that he was really pleased. 'Congratulations, well done, I'm so pleased for you,' I said. He immediately said, 'No, for us.' Then he had to go back in to the meeting.

After this piece of news, I put the mop down and made a cup of tea. After the last eight months of hell, I was very excited and happy for Terry. It finally seemed as if our luck was turning for the better.

When we got in at about nine o'clock, we had dinner and chatted about the day. By the time we went to bed my mind was racing and I couldn't sleep. I began to feel very mixed emotions. Part of me was glad he had the job but part of me was dreading being back in the public eye. I felt anxious and concerned about the future. I have to admit that for the first time in a long while I cried silently into my pillow as Terry slept beside me. But I knew that it was too late to look back. For better or for worse our great adventure had begun.

The next day I woke up feeling much better and more positive about everything. I went into Scribes and a lot of people came in to offer their congratulations. In the morning Terry went off to a meeting with Stephanie Moore at West Ham football club, regarding a memorial match for our good friend, Bobby. West Ham were planning a special match, and Stephanie had requested that a quarter of all proceeds to go to the Bobby Moore Fund for Imperial Cancer Research. It's nice to think that Bobby's memory will live on through important research into the causes and cures of colon cancer. He and Stephanie were very close friends of ours and his death was a loss we all felt very deeply.

In the evening we went out to dinner at L'Incontro – Gino Santin's restaurant – with our friends Bobby and Jan Keetch. It had been a difficult year for Gino, who saw his reputation torn apart in the *Panorama* programme, for which he was later awarded substantial damages from the BBC. He was delighted about Terry getting the England job and celebrated with us.

However, the really emotional moment for me was the next day, when I saw the television pictures of Terry standing on the Wembley pitch with his arms outstretched and 'Congratulations, good luck, Terry' on the electronic scoreboard. After all the months of pain and aggravation here was the final moment of triumph.

I went to Scribes later on and the place was stacked high with cards, flowers and champagne, and was full of people waiting to congratulate Terry. It was wonderful. I really felt as if a new chapter was starting in our lives. That night we went to dinner to Montpeliano's and finished the day shattered but very happy.

Terry went to the FA for the first time as England Coach on Monday 31 January, 1994. I felt as though I was sending a kid off to his new school. As he left he said to me, 'This can't be me, you know. It doesn't feel right.' I just said, 'You'll be all right once you get there.'

But when he came back to meet me at Scribes later that day his first impressions hadn't been very positive. I could see he was unsure about the FA. The second day was better and after he'd been introduced to all the FA's employees he cheered up. He thought they all seemed nice people and would be good to work with. And so began his new life as England Coach.

# CHAPTER ONE

## THE NEW BOY

To be coach of the England football team is the dream of everybody seriously involved in football. That is until reality sets in. When you really think about it, it is a difficult job. Graham Taylor called it the 'impossible job', and it is. It's not well paid and the odds on actually winning something are slim as there are so many other factors which influence the job, and which are completely beyond the control of the manager or coach.

But having said that, you always think you will be the one to beat the odds, pull off the impossible dream and win a major tournament. Like everyone else who has gone before me, I thought I could be the one to achieve success. Also, being England Coach is the pinnacle from which you can view the game, both nationally and internationally. So, it was with immense pride and pleasure that my dream came true and the announcement was made of my appointment.

Friday 28 January, 1994 was one of the greatest days of my life. It's a day I'll never forget, not only because it was the end of weeks of speculation, but also because of the publicity surrounding my appearance as the new England Coach at Wembley stadium. As I walked out into the winter sunshine, the flash from the photographers' cameras was blinding. There must have been about seventy photographers and they all wanted a different angle of me, so it was a case of 'This way Terry. No, over here, to the left, look this way' and so on for about half an hour.

This was followed by a press conference and another interminable round of interviews for the television and radio journalists. I started to understand just how much press attention the job attracts but Barcelona's media coverage held me in good stead for this extravaganza. But finally it was all over and I had officially been crowned England Coach. As people went off to celebrate, I drove back to Scribes happy but shattered, for what I thought would be a quiet drink with my family and friends. But as I walked in, the place was packed with friends and well-wishers and so we had another noisy celebration which lasted well into the night, and then Yvette and I slipped away to Montpeliano.

Like some of the major football clubs, joining the FA is like being part of history. The Football Association actually came into being on 26 October, 1863, when a meeting of the leading clubs and schools playing the sport decided to co-operate in framing a unified set of official rules under which everyone could play.

This meeting was held at the Freemason's Tavern in Great Queen Street, London, and the clubs that were represented were: Barnes; Blackheath; Charterhouse, Perceval House (Blackheath); Kensington School; War Office; Crystal Palace; Blackheath Proprietary School; The Crusaders; Forest (Leytonstone) and No Names (Kilburn).

It took five meetings before the laws of the game could be agreed. Shortly afterwards Blackheath withdrew from membership because they opposed the law banning hacking (uncontrolled kicking). The other early controversy concerned the offside law and it was not until 1867 that the new law obtained general acceptance.

The decision that did most to promote the sport's development came on July 20, 1871 when it was proposed that a Challenge Cup be established for competition among members. The FA Challenge Cup is the oldest competition in the world game – and also one of the most famous and prestigious.

With all this history and a strong element of an old boys' club pervading the corridors of power, it is no wonder that the FA has sometimes suffered from rather a fuddy duddy image. It hasn't been easy to pull itself into the high tech, commercially pressurized world that we live in, but there are real signs of a desire to lead world football into the twenty-first century.

When I finally arrived at the FA, I had discussed my position at length with the chairman, Sir Bert Millichip and chief executive, Graham Kelly and understood that my primary role at the FA would be as England Coach. It was made clear that nobody would interfere in my decisions related to this job. As I sat and thought about the future, and what I wanted to achieve, four very clear objectives came to mind:

1. I want to build a strong England team and implement a system that will carry us through to the next century.
2. I want to lead the England team to success in the European Championship finals in the summer of 1996 and on to the World Cup.
3. I want to create a link between the professional game and the interests of the FA. I think there is too much of a gap between the various leagues and the FA. We should be communicating with one another and ensuring there is some kind of consistency in the game. It is in the interests of everyone if we can learn how to help each other. For example, it is in our interests to suspend league games on the weekend before an England match; in exchange maybe it is in their interests if we can help them in Europe by exchanging our experiences of playing against foreign sides.
   Everyone who is involved in the game wants to see English clubs do well, whether it is the England team playing or an English side playing against a European side in a cup match. It is time we built bridges rather than hide behind a cloak of unnecessary secrecy.
4. I would also like to make the game more cohesive and build on what we have. At present many of the Under-21 players don't go on to make the senior side, and I think this is wrong. I feel that promising young players should have an early introduction to the senior side, just to see how it works and to learn from the experience of the older players. This also applies to the 15- and 16-year-olds and the Under-18s. I see little point in constantly chopping and changing, introducing new, different players when, with a little forward planning, we can have interesting, young talent from the youth sides.

Apart from my responsibilities as England Coach, I will also sit on the International Committee, and report to the members. The chairman of this committee is Noel White of Liverpool. I'm also on the Technical Board.

In the light of all the false allegations laid at my door after my departure from Tottenham, a lot of people have asked me if I was forced to take on the title of England Coach as opposed to England Manager, which was the title given to all my predecessors. The answer to that is an unequivocal No! I think that people who know me, or even half know me, have realized by now that I can't be forced to agree to anything that is unfair. That may of course, have been in the minds of my interviewers, but it wasn't mentioned to me. It was just that it was suggested to me that coach may be a more appropriate title. The manager of Spain or Italy is the national team coach, not manager, and it just makes more sense. The role is one of a coach not a manager. There's no general administration or contract work involved, just the skill of picking the best players available and coaching them for the games.

After the announcement, it was just a case of settling into my office at the Football Association and getting on with things. I felt that out of the four objectives my priority was to make the England team a major force on the world stage once more. Over the last few years we'd taken a bit of a battering and, having missed out on the World Cup in America, we were not commanding the same level of respect that we should have been enjoying. Foreign teams no longer thought of us as tough opponents, and psychologically that was bad news.

There's a photograph hanging on the wall of the FA that sums it all up. It is of the late, great Bobby Moore, pictured standing at Wembley. He's dressed in the England strip, holding the ball and looking out into the distance with an expression on his face that captures the pride and honour that used to come from being chosen to play for your country. He looks like a latter-day Greek god and must have been frightening for the opposition.

I wanted England players to feel like that again. They need confidence and pride in themselves and I considered it an important part of my job to instil those qualities in the players who would represent England.

But the first task was to choose my coaching staff. I wanted a good combination of experience and youthfulness. I wanted there to be consistency in the game instead of the constant change that we'd seen in recent years. Every time someone new had come in there'd been a clean sweep of the board and they'd followed the 'let's start anew' policy.

But that's not always the best philosophy. Experience counts in this game. Men who have come up through the ranks and seen the pros and cons of certain situations are as invaluable as the fresh talent that comes on board with its own ideas and new methods. So I chose Don Howe and Bryan Robson to back me up with the senior team and Ray Wilkins to come in with the Under-21s. Don's experience was very important, but I thought we needed someone who was closer in age to the players, and this is where Bryan came in. Not only has he been a top class player and England captain, but he is a very steady person. His calming influence combined with his ability to command respect is ideal for us, and I want to involve him in all the team strategy and planning for the future. Don's role is essentially as technical co-ordinator. He acts as a link between Charles Hughes, who is in charge of all coaching apart from the England teams, and the coaches of the Under-18s, the Under-17s and the other England teams.

I also appointed Dave Butler and Alan Smith as the two England physios. Dave has worked with me at Tottenham, QPR and Crystal Palace and is highly experienced and competent, and Alan Smith is a talented down-to-earth Yorkshireman. I thought that the two previous physios, Fred Street and Norman Medhurst, did a very good job and they were both utterly dedicated to England, but in this department it was time for a change. We needed a new dash of enthusiasm and fresh ideas.

The other new appointment that I made was to bring in Ted Buxton, who had also worked with me at Tottenham as a scout. When I arrived at the FA I was astounded to discover that there was practically no information about international teams and players. It's the age of the computer and yet here we were scrabbling around trying to get an informed opinion about past games and the opposing team's players, particularly those who had caused us problems or been outstanding in some way. There wasn't even a library of videos of past games so we couldn't assess any problems, or the progress made over the years.

Ted has a particular gifted eye for picking out potential problem players and assessing players in general. It was obvious we desperately needed a man like Ted on board. I gave him the job as my assistant, which in real terms means chief scout. That involves travelling around England and the world, reporting on players and teams and building up our own information library.

These are the people who assist me on the pitch, but I also have a team to help me in the office.

The England Coach's office is situated on the third floor of the English Football Association, at 16 Lancaster Gate, Bayswater, London. As you walk through the doors there is the hallowed, quiet atmosphere of tradition. The trophy cabinet on the left-hand wall is full of silver cups and medals illustrating the long and extremely successful history of the England team. As you move through the heavy mahogany doors to the lift, there are constant reminders of the great tradition of the FA. Photographs of outstanding players and managers hang side by side with photographs of great games like England v Brazil in the 1970 World Cup, and more recently England v Germany in the semi-finals of the 1990 World Cup in Italy, as well as a selection of colour portraits of our boys in action.

The lift glides up to the third floor, and you go through a set of double doors, turn right and there is my team. My secretary, Frances has a desk which faces my office and she is responsible for all national business. She keeps tabs on my appointments in England, organizes the Under-21s and arranges tickets for the matches I want to see in this country, as well as ensuring I meet my commitments with the England team.

Michelle is my international secretary. She not only organizes my trips abroad to see England players, but is also responsible for liaising with our opposition. She travels with the team and is charged with the awesome task of ensuring that, administratively speaking, nothing goes wrong. Michelle and Frances are both highly capable.

As well as the girls in the office, the other vital link in my job is David Davies, Director of Public Affairs for the FA. David arrived at the same time as me and deals with the media, which is not an easy task. He arranges the press conferences and sets up the individual meetings with various journalists who request to see me. Fortunately, David and I hit it off straight away and we have a very good working relationship, which is vital for us both.

I find it sad that, like most Premier League managers, I can't air my thoughts on what I think about my players at the general press conferences. I always find myself in the middle of the war between the *Sun* and the *Mirror,* who each have to out-sensationalize the other in an attempt to win readers. For example, a remark like

'Smith's form is not so good at the moment' could turn into a headline like 'Smith will not play for England again'. This means that I have to spend more time than usual with individual journalists talking on a one-to-one basis to ensure that everyone gets enough information.

As I sat in my office during the first couple of weeks of February, 1994, I asked myself some searching questions. The most pertinent of these was simply, Could we win the European Championships? One of the big pluses is that the finals are in England, and although it has been twelve years since the host nation won a major international tournament (when France won the European Championships in 1984) this must be an advantage as we don't have to qualify. But the downside to this is that while other teams are qualifying we have to try to find useful opposition to play against.

And this was my second disappointment. I was shocked to find out that even though England was appointed host nation for the European Championship finals in May 1992, there were very few games organized in the run-up to the tournament. This showed a lack of forward thinking on the part of the FA. I was not impressed.

However, the FA's Commercial Director, Trevor Phillips was soon in action and pulled off the coup of negotiating for three of the world's top teams to play in the 1995 Umbro mini-tournament. We had Japan, Sweden, who are number three in the world, and the World Cup holders, Brazil. Not bad! And it would give me a chance to see just how much progress the England team had made since I had become England Coach. It was also a chance for the FA to be commercially aware. The Football Association only earns a certain percentage of the profits from the European Championship finals, but money made from the 1995 tournament would stay in England and be ploughed back into the game. It would be an important dress rehearsal for Euro 96 both on and off the pitch.

At the same time that I asked myself if we could win the tournament, I also had to ask if we are technically gifted enough to win it, or are other countries better equipped technically speaking, and if so why? I thought about this and made several lists of English talent and decided we had enough players who had both ability and determination to make us not only a strong contender, but also give us a chance of finishing in the top six.

The one thing that did concern me was how I could develop team play in such a short time. I knew that without team play we couldn't win the European Championships. You just can't build a team round one player. To put something so vast round one or two individuals is suicidal. Carlos Alberto Parreira, the Brazilian national team coach, says that, 'The star of the team must be the whole team.' And I agree with him. When he won the World Cup in 1994, he did it with a talented but disciplined team, and that was the difference from previous years. In the 70s talent and sheer ability was enough to win major tournaments. Think back to the outstanding Brazilian teams of the 60s and 70s. They were little more than a group of incredibly talented players enjoying playing football in the way they knew best. It was inspiring and beautiful to watch, but by the mid-80s rhythm and beauty were not enough against the more drilled skills of teams like Germany. And so Brazil stopped winning. Carlos Parreira had to put discipline and organization into his team. Against public opinion he built a team that could, and did, win the World Cup.

Carlos Parreira is one of the international coaches that I admire most, and I knew that listening to him talk, at a UEFA seminar, about his experiences would be invaluable. His job as national team coach of Brazil is more pressurized than mine! He said that if he had lost the World Cup, he couldn't have gone home for three or four months.

But back in England, as I sat in my office mulling things over, I knew we had big problems which, if we didn't address now, would lead to a further demise of England on the international stage. We had no clear-cut policy to reach the seven-year-olds and get them enthusiastic about the game of football. I thought a valid youth policy was vital for the future. After all, if we don't invest in the future eventually kids will turn to alternatives like participating in shows like *Gladiators* and football will become that 'funny old game that grandpa used to play'.

Unlike a lot of my contemporaries, I have been fortunate to have been the coach of a foreign team. My time with Barcelona gave me the invaluable experience of being able to observe how another nation lives, and a part of that observation was watching the kids play. I know the weather has something to do with it, but the young Spanish kids were forever out and about kicking a ball, either in their own back yards or on the beach, and this not only gave them enthusiasm for the game, but also gave them a head start in the skills stakes. Scandinavian countries don't have the good weather, but have good indoor facilities. We have neither.

When I was a kid I used to kick a ball around with friends, but nowadays it is difficult for kids to do this. A lot of our playing fields have been sold off (more of this later) and there just aren't the facilities for playing team sport at schools. It was at this point that I decided I had an important fifth objective, and that was to use my position to encourage the Government, the FA and industry to invest in the future by providing kids with basic facilities like playing fields and equipment.

The other big thing that was more directly connected to our international demise was the long ban on English clubs competing in Europe. I'm not criticizing the ban, just looking at the reasons why we hadn't performed well; and part of the reason has to be because clubs like Liverpool, who had consistently been in the European Cup, were no longer coming up against the best of Europe. In a technical sense, we were becoming isolated. As the other clubs who competed in European competitions were constantly evolving, we were being left behind.

At club level in the 80s we were starting to play the long, direct style of play to the exclusion of skill. Fortunately in latter years this has been compensated for to some degree by the emergence of the School of Excellence at Lilleshall. Andy Cole, the first seven million pound player, went through it, as did at least six of the Tottenham players who during my time at the club went on to play in the first team. Although the school has its successes, it only deals with progress in a very small target area. Only 16 boys qualify each year – which is why we call it the School of Excellence. However, we also have to provide the same opportunity across the country to enable all youngsters to enjoy similar facilities.

As I started scribbling notes, I decided to do some immediate research on what was wrong and what was right with the England team.

I spoke to Lawrie McMenemy, my predecessor Graham Taylor's number two, who was very helpful. He was very bullish about the whole thing and we went over quite a few points. One of the problems was the length of the training sessions. If the team were together over a six-day period it meant that they were together for the weekend, and the players found it difficult to be away for so long. The foreign players are used to it, as I found at Barcelona. If you explain to them that they need to be together to build team loyalty and be isolated from outside pressures before a game, they will settle down, accept it and read a book or watch television. In Spain this time is called 'concentration'. In England players get bored, and if they get bored it is a problem, as it starts to take the edge off their game. Organized entertainments, such as trips to the theatre or meals out, have never gone down that well.

So I decided to change things a bit. We could still have Thursday night, Friday and Saturday morning together, then I'd let them off until Sunday night, when they'd come back ready for Monday. We'd have Monday and Tuesday training and then Wednesday would be match day. This would relieve the problem of keeping morale high.

I did have a chat to Sir Alf Ramsey. He came down to Scribes and we talked about how things had changed since the 1966 days. We agreed that tactically speaking, the gap has narrowed between the teams of established nations, and the younger emerging sides of Asia and Africa.

The first match I went to as England Coach was at Loftus Road: QPR v Manchester Utd on Saturday 5 February. I was touched to receive a standing ovation as I took my seat. I thought it was a good start, that the crowd were on my side. Unfortunately it wasn't such a good day for QPR, who lost 2–3 to United. The United defence was excellent, but the match was a good example of a classic English, fast, furious attacking game, and the fans were rewarded with five goals.

As well as beginning to shape things in the Venables mould, I also had to get a team together for the first friendly match, against current European Champions Denmark. My first priority was to check on two key players — David Platt and Paul Gascoigne. So I took the plane to Rome and called in on Gazza.

The Press asked if they could come along to witness the reunion between me and Gazza. I agreed, and we arrived in a blaze of publicity. I went to watch Gazza play and he was in good spirits. He had a very good game, he was the instigator of a lot of action and gave us a demonstration of his great one-touch passes. I was pleased for him. Afterwards he seemed in good form, full of himself and laughing and joking. The next day we arranged to meet for lunch, but meanwhile the Press asked me if I'd go to dinner with them. I said yes just as long as Harry Harris wasn't included in the group. Harry Harris is the *Mirror*'s main football man and has been a constant thorn in my side during all the business with Alan Sugar. He has tried everything to discredit me and I didn't feel I could be a hypocrite and sit down at the same table as if nothing had happened.

He protested that the England Coach shouldn't be able to choose who he has dinner with, but I said, 'No. I'm just choosing who I won't have dinner with!'

The next day, I met Gazza at the magnificent Hassler Hotel, which stands at the top of the Spanish Steps in Rome. I have to say that I was impressed with him. I've known Gazza for many years, ever since he played at Tottenham, and I know his way of doing things and how he thinks. Some people, including Gazza, have said that I'm his second dad, which is a great compliment as players with Gazza's talent are very rare. It's just a case of getting the best out of him. He needs a firm hand but he needs freedom too and you have to know when to slap his wrists and when to give him a free rein, both on and off the pitch. It had been a while since I had last seen him, and he seemed to have grown up a bit. There was a new maturity as he talked about his experiences in Italy. I thought the new surroundings would be good for him. I'd have liked to have seen how he would have done with another season in Italy now he was fit.

Gazza's had his problems, like injuries and various highly publicized mishaps away from the football pitch, but you can't keep him down for long. His passion and love of the game have always kept him going through the tough times. It all turned into a bit of a madhouse in Rome, with endless photographs and an impromptu press conference, but I left Gazza in good spirits.

Finally, I flew off to Genoa to see David Platt. When I landed, the difference between the two cities of Rome and Genoa couldn't have been more apparent. David was waiting to meet me at the airport on his own, with no fans bothering him. He was treated just like any other bloke, unlike Gazza down in Rome.

In spite of David's illustrious career at club and international level, we had never actually met. So this was a get-to-know-you meeting. David is one of the few players who doesn't have a problem with being away from home in the training camp, but he agreed that the enforced entertainment wasn't working. There was no point in going out just for the sake of it. He didn't really dwell too much on the previous England set-up and that suited me fine. I wanted to get to know David and have a light-hearted chat.

Along with Gary Lineker, David is an example of a player who is maximizing his potential. His attitude is spot on and others should be encouraged to follow his example. He speaks Italian and says he wants to be a team manager in Italy when he finishes his playing career. I think this is another example of how we should be encouraging kids from seven upwards to not only play team games but also to have a broader outlook on life which fits in with being part of Europe and not just an island.

In Spain and Italy, where there is still a strong family unit, they have a stronger sense of family values and learn to respect their elders and reap benefits through hard work. Just when they may go astray young adults spend a year in the army, and that sorts them out. I think this type of lifestyle is good for the future of our society. The Government has a 'back to basics campaign', but it is of little use if there aren't any tangible measures being taken to implement it.

Kids have to be led and educated to protect their talent, not stifle it. I believe it is important to get kids involved in the game when they are young and before they get too influenced by their neighbourhood culture. If you get them young enough, you can minimize the damage caused by a reckless personality, and the coach can help mould their personality in a healthy and responsible manner.

I returned from Italy feeling confident that I'd renewed my close relationship with Gazza, and started to get to know the man who would be my new captain. Both players are key members of the England set-up, although as I've already said, it is never a good idea to rely too heavily on one player as injury or other circumstances can change things very quickly.

But at the end of my first month I was feeling optimistic about the future. The next challenge was whether I could put words into action and produce a team that would be able to take on the European Champions.

# CHAPTER TWO

## THE FIRST MATCH

My job is to select players who are the best players to play for England. This doesn't necessarily mean the most talented. Some players are very talented but are nervous when putting on an England shirt. It's like a player moving from a club such as Bristol Rovers to Manchester United. When he pulls on the United shirt and prepares to run out on to the pitch for his first game, he is either peering nervously round the dressing-room door, or strutting proudly forward ready to take on the challenge.

I had to decide who was up to the job. I wanted to get our confidence back and I wanted to make immediate progress, so I had my eye on players like Darren Anderton and Graeme Le Saux. I felt that as well as being outstanding players they were intelligent and could pick things up quickly. I also wanted David Platt and Alan Shearer who I thought would be useful not only because of their ability, but because they would be a steady influence on the team.

### The Squad
David Seaman – Arsenal
Tim Flowers – Blackburn Rovers
Paul Parker – Manchester United
Rob Jones – Liverpool
Stuart Pearce – Nottingham Forest
Graeme Le Saux – Blackburn Rovers
Tony Adams – Arsenal
Gary Pallister – Manchester United

Des Walker – Sheffield Wednesday
Darren Anderton – Tottenham Hotspur
Paul Gascoigne – Lazio
Paul Ince – Manchester United
David Batty – Blackburn Rovers
David Platt – Sampdoria
Matthew Le Tissier – Southampton
Alan Shearer – Blackburn Rovers
Les Ferdinand – Queen's Park Rangers
Peter Beardsley – Newcastle United
Ian Wright – Arsenal

And then once I'd decided who could do the job it was back to strategy. I had to modify the old traditional way of playing the 4-4-2 formation. By using this system we were solving the opposition's problems. We just had to ask more questions of the opposition to give us a good platform from which to play.

Under the old system we played two wingers wide and used two strikers up front. All the opposition had to do was put the two full-backs on our wingers and send their centre-halves out to mark our strikers. Add the sweeper and they'd solved their main problems before they'd even got on the pitch. We used to withdraw wide players, but I wanted a lot of width.

So to make things more difficult, I devised a new system: the Christmas tree (see opposite). I changed the basic shape of the team so that instead of having two strikers up front, I put one up front with two just behind, three players in midfield and four at the back.

So against Denmark, I had Shearer up front with Beardsley and Platt just behind him. In midfield, I had Anderton on the right, Paul Ince in the middle and Gazza on the left. The back four were Le Saux, Gary Pallister, Tony Adams and Paul Parker, with David Seaman in goal. This would give the opposition problems in that the centre-halves wouldn't be sure who to mark or whether to pull their midfield back.

My two main objectives on the first morning of training at Burnham Beeches were to instil confidence into the players and get a good result against the reigning European Champions.

As we got stuck into our training programme, I had already decided that I would limit the 'classroom' lessons. It is easy to start using the blackboard to explain your tactics, but as I didn't know

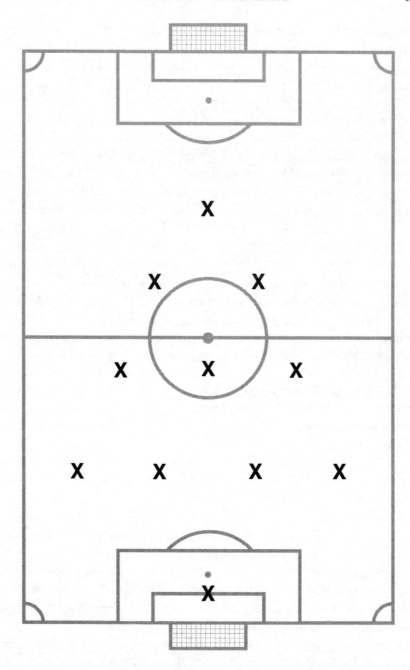

**England's 'Christmas Tree' formation**

the players I didn't want to create confusion. The disadvantage
with using a blackboard is that it can look as if you expect more
from the players than you actually have in mind, and that can cause
damage as it frightens the players and then they get a mental block
trying to remember if they are doing everything they think they are
supposed to do.

Even if we can only have a short time on the pitch, I prefer to
do my work on it and lead by practical example. I can then say
things like: 'When the ball is here, you've got to be there,' and
they can see where I am pointing to, and when that situation arises
in a game they know exactly what is expected of them. Whereas if
it had only been explained on a blackboard, there is always the
chance that the player is left thinking: 'Did he mean there or over
somewhere else?' Some players understand board work better than
others, but most players respond well on the pitch.

My number one motto in training is KEEP THINGS SIMPLE.

When I'm working with other coaches I will revert to blackboard work as they are used to playing around with various tactical
systems, but the players are often used to using their talent in a
very straightforward way without thinking too hard about what
they are doing. I've sometimes seen a world class striker hesitate in
front of the goal before shooting, and missing the target. This is
often because instead of doing it instinctively, he pauses to think
for a minute and the chance is lost.

I felt really good about being back in football; I love the game,
I always have and I always will, and to be involved in coaching
again made me very happy.

During those first few days at Burnham Beeches I also wanted
to create a fun, relaxed atmosphere. If the results haven't been
good the players are generally low in confidence, so you have to try
and pick them up, whereas if you are at the top of the league you
have to make sure they don't get over-confident. My philosophy in
life, as well as in football, is to try and follow a straight line. If
things go wrong you shouldn't lose sight of the overall objective
and stray too far off the line to pull things back, and if things go
really well you shouldn't go too far the other way and burn yourself out by celebrating. You should always have that line in front of
you to guide you.

I was really delighted by the players' performance on the pitch
during training and, later, during the match. The two players just

behind Shearer – Beardsley and Platt – picked up their new roles very quickly and very efficiently. Gazza and Anderton had to provide a link between attack and midfield, and that is just what they did, getting forward into the box when the opportunity arose, and then dropping back to add weight to the midfield.

I was very lucky in this first match as I had my first-choice players available to me — there were no drop outs through injury or other commitments.

As Anderton was going to break wide on the right a lot of the time, Platt could stay quite central, and break with Gazza into the box. So I asked Beardsley to go wide, cover the left wing, and link up with Shearer on that side. That meant that we had a natural balance on the right and a slightly more forced, but nevertheless effective, balance on the left.

If Beardsley went wide, you'd have Shearer and Platt getting into the box, and on the other side when Anderton got the ball Beardsley or Gascoigne would play forward into the box with Shearer, or whoever is nearest to him.

Something else that I had to take into consideration was the fact that we were very likely to only have 20 players – 21 with the extra goalkeeper – for Euro 96. That's 18 outfield players. They did this in 1992, but they had one round less, as from the three-game play-off, they went straight into the semi-finals and then the final. In 1994, the number reverted back to 22, but if UEFA decided on the 20 man squad for 1996, that would mean five games plus the Final. They came to this decision as 23 players would mean one official less, so that there was space on the bench for the extra player. This possibility changed my attitude when forming the squad, as you have to consider how flexible a player is and whether he can play in different positions. You can't have a team full of specialists. If I wanted to play with two wide players on the wings, then I'd have to have three wide players in the squad. However, if two of these players got injured, then I'd have to change my system, so I was aware from day one that I would have to play around with tactics until I got the right combination of ability and flexibility.

A lot of people are interested to know more about the vital role of one of the key members of the England team – the team doctor. Doctor John Crane has been involved with the Football Association since 1978, when he looked after the Under-21s.

**England's formation versus Denmark, Greece and Norway**

◀---- Shows player movement

From 1986, he has been the doctor for the first team. He is an absolutely vital link in our preparations as he is the one who decides if the players are fit to train and play, and he also decides on treatment and sets the rules on diet. He has one big defect – he's an Arsenal supporter, but I won't hold that against him. We were together when the Under-21s won the European Championship and I was coach with Dave Sexton. I used to kid the doctor about him working with Arsenal. But after what happened at Spurs, I like Arsenal too!

The doc, like most of us, arrives before the players get to the hotel. His first day is spent assessing the injured players and deciding if they can stay with us or not. It is always possible that the injury is worse than previously thought, and then we have to decide whether to send the player back to his club. Our policy is to send unfit players back to their clubs so that they can have continuous treatment from the club doctors.

The week before we get to the training camp, the doc has discussed all the menus with the hotel and decided what we will eat. The main purpose is to feed the players with a high carbohydrate diet and keep the fat content down to about 15 per cent of the total intake. That means the players can eat chips, which have been cut chunkily and so do not absorb too much fat, like the ones we serve at Scribes, rather than the thin hamburger-joint varieties.

Whilst in the training camp, the doctor liaises with the physios, Dave Butler and Alan Smith, as to what type of treatment the injured players should have and the frequency of treatment.

Then of course we have to take into consideration the conditions in which we are playing. As Dr Crane says, 'If the team is playing in a hot country or at high altitude, we have to make allowances. If we are playing at height, then we always have to ensure we train at a higher level, as the haemoglobin level in the blood has to adjust and compensate for less oxygen in the atmosphere. Obviously if there is a combination of heat and humidity then the players have to increase their fluid intake. We need at least two weeks to acclimatize to playing, for example, in Mexico or one of the South American countries. We deploy all sorts of tactics to make the body adjust quicker, such as training with loads of clothes on. This brings little-used sweat glands into use far quicker than just waiting for them to start working under normal conditions.'

The physios report to the doctor on a daily basis, and the doctor reports to me first thing in the morning so that I am kept up to
date on the severity or improvement of the injuries. The doctor
reckons I am more probing than some of my predecessors, but
that is because I want to be informed and I want to be able to
explain things fully to the club managers. If a player picks up an
injury with us, then I need to explain in some detail what it means
and what we are doing. The doc specializes in sports medicine,
which means that he is aware of a sports person's needs. You have
to assess the injury in the light of the fact that the player probably
has better overall fitness than the average person, and also take into
consideration the requirements of the muscles that are used. For
example, a simple knock or a bruised muscle will heal, for a footballer, in one or two days, as long as the bruise isn't inside the
muscle.

The doc has seen a lot of action with England and I was curious on this first get together to know what were his best memories
of the job. He said, 'The best moments for me are always as we
walk out on to the pitch before a match. The colour and noise of
the crowd is uplifting, and to walk out before a World Cup match
is even more special. I loved the atmosphere in Italy during the
1990 World Cup. The whole country loves football and gave itself
over to enjoying the great carnival that is the World Cup. The
food was also very good for the players. We had a very enjoyable
time: the team did exceptionally well in reaching the semi-finals,
and we all came away feeling it had been a very satisfactory few
weeks.'

'Did you have any amusing incidents along the way?' I asked. I
was curious to know what the players got up to when they are
away at a major tournament.

The doc smiled. 'We used to play golf at our team hotel in
Cagliari, the Is. Moras. A tournament was organized to provide
some light relief for the players before the last two matches of our
group. Bobby Robson enjoyed a game of golf and took the tournament seriously, so the lads decided to play a trick on him and
substitute his golf ball with an exploding variety. When Bobby
teed off on the tenth hole he got the shock of his life as his golf ball
disintegrated in a ball of white dust!

'During the same tournament I accidently took Bobby
Robson's kit bag, and he was left with kit that was too big for him.

I'm an extra large. So Bobby had to go around with his sleeves hanging down round his knees, much to the amusement of the players and staff. However, it's important to keep a relaxed and happy atmosphere, especially when you are away from home for up to two months. If the players start to bitch and fight then the team spirit will break down, so Bobby was more than happy to be the butt of jokes.'

Did you have any problems amongst the players? I was looking for any problem personalities.

'No, it was a remarkably cohesive group. Gazza was one of the more ebullient members, but he was a new boy and so was kept under control by the more experienced players. We had a brilliant captain in Bryan Robson. Bryan went out of his way to ensure that everything ran smoothly. If there were any little upsets in Cagliari he would speak to the players concerned in a quiet and firm manner, and they would immediately settle down.'

As well as all the innocent fun, I remember that there were some less funny moments, including the accusation that several England team members had taken part in some kind of sex romp with a World Cup hostess. The doc reassured me that this was another fabrication by the Press. However, some of the tensest moments both before and after Italia 90 had not been witnessed by the media.

In other tournaments, Terry Butcher seems to have been in the wrong place at the wrong time on a couple of occasions, and even managed to change the rules.

'Terry picked up a laceration to his scalp during a European qualifying match for the 1992 finals in Sweden and as he insisted on carrying on, I stitched him up at half-time, even though there was still blood pouring down his face. It was also raining and I can assure you that it was a hell of a sight. There was so much blood around that when he headed the ball back to our goalkeeper, the ball stuck to the goalie's hands! The whole match was turned into a blood bath and the officials watching it decided that this kind of thing had to be stopped. So it was shortly after this that UEFA passed a rule stating that no one was allowed on the pitch if they were bleeding.

'The other very tense moment was after Maradona's "Hand of God" incident, which effectively knocked us out of the 1986 World Cup. After the match Terry Butcher was like an over-wound spring. He was so furious he couldn't even speak. And then he was called in for an anti-doping test. I accompanied him, as the team doctor has to wait with the player in the allocated room until he can give a urine sample. This can take up to four hours if he is very dehydrated! We were sitting there silently while Terry contemplated the unfairness of it all, when who should walk in from the Argentinian team but Maradona who had also been selected for anti-doping! Talk about a charged atmosphere. Terry sat there glowering at his rival, while Maradona chatted and giggled and was full of the joys of spring. I was silently praying that Maradona wouldn't make any funny jokes, as I thought I would have to physically restrain Terry from clocking him one. But fortunately, Maradona managed to give his sample after five minutes and was gone, whereas Terry and I sat there for nearly an hour before he could give his.'

All I could think of as I was listening to the doc recounting this story was how pleased I was that the team manager didn't have to be in there as well, or we would have risked seriously damaging the already fragile relationship between Argentina and the United Kingdom. Whoever decided on the players for the drugs test must have been a diplomat!

The doc's job is a very important one, especially with all the complications of banned drugs. The list just seems to get longer. Dr Crane is responsible for seeing all fifteen players, that is the team plus reserves, as soon as they arrive at the venue in which they will play. He then has to write down *all* the drugs or medicines they have taken over the last seventy-two hours. As Dr Crane says, 'This is a great worry, as there are so many over-the-counter drugs that are banned it's very easy to fall into a trap. The list includes medicines used by asthmatics, such as Ventolin, so if you have an asthmatic player, he has to be automatically declared asthmatic to the authorities, even if it is a temporary condition. Some cold and cough medicines are banned, as well as the old fashioned barbiturate sleeping drugs and beta-blockers, which people often take to calm down before an exam. But they are prohibited as they make players feel calm and in control, and could improve performance during a penalty shoot-out.' Maybe the managers and their wives could have them instead!

The doctor has to take a wide range of drugs with him whenever England are at home or away. These range from anti-diarrhoea mixture to a heart resuscitator. If there is a serious injury the doctor has back-up help from Mr Stephen Cannon, who is an orthopaedic surgeon from the Royal Orthopaedic Hospital. He offers a second opinion and takes over if surgery is required.

Before we broke up and went off to chase up the players, Dr Crane had one final funny story to tell me.

'I think the most amusing incident that ever happened in my time as team doctor was when the team was playing in Romania some years ago. It was the pre-match meal, and I decided to order baked beans on toast for the players, as baked beans are rich in carbohydrates. So I took the tins of baked beans into the kitchen (up until the fall of the Berlin Wall the team used to bring their own food with them when they travelled behind the Iron Curtain) and asked the chef to serve them up. Ten or fifteen minutes went by and I walked into the dining room before the players arrived, and to my great surprise was confronted with a sea of plates on which stood the tins of baked beans, unopened and cold. I went back into the kitchen and asked the chef to heat them up. They re-emerged a few minutes later, with the labels and tops off, still in the tins but this time they were hot!

'We couldn't contemplate an alternative as it was almost time to board the team coach to go to the stadium for the match. So I went back to the kitchen having decided to simplify matters and order an easy to prepare omelette to eat with the baked beans. I made sure that the chef understood that the baked beans had to be taken out of the tins.

'Another ten minutes or so passed, and then with a dramatic flourish the doors opened and in came the biggest omelette I have ever seen; I couldn't even get my arms round it. Instead of cooking individual omelettes with baked beans on the side the chef had made one enormous omelette and cooked all the beans inside it. Although I was taken aback by this, the players were delighted and voted it the best pre-match meal they had ever eaten!'

I enjoyed talking to John Crane and then sat back and thought about my routine at the training camp.

A typical day for me at Bisham Abbey is one in which the needs of the media have to be considered. You can't simply say, 'Come in and do your photos and interviews today, and then tomorrow let me have a day alone with the players'. The media all want

something everyday. So on the Monday before the Denmark
game, for example, we left the hotel at Burnham Beeches at nine-
thirty in the morning, and got to Bisham Abbey at ten to ten.
Then we started the training session at ten. The photographers
wanted their photos of the players training, so I let them in at
eleven-thirty.

We had a break at eleven forty-five for coffee, and resumed
training at twelve-thirty. But in that forty-five minute break I had
to go and talk to the Press, along with the two players nominated
by the journalists. We have to do the television interviews, and
there are normally about three television stations. Then we have
to do about six radio interviews, all separately, before going on to
talk to the daily papers, of which there are about thirty, and finally
the Sunday papers. You have to break off from concentrating with
the players on the pitch to do all this. It's very intense work over a
very short period of time. It would make life a lot easier if we
could just concentrate on training but dealing with the media is
part of the job and it is important to keep the public as well
informed as possible.

Don Howe was amazed at the number of Press who turned up.
He said that the number of journalists had at least doubled since
he was with Bobby Robson during Italia 90. I have asked for the
FA to implement a system of accreditation for the media at Bisham
Abbey, as anyone can wander in and out, and apart from the regu-
lars, half the time you don't even know who everyone is. The main
problem is you can't spread this interview session out as all the
media people have their deadlines to reach and the afternoon is
too late for them. So we all dash about trying to get it all done in
the allotted time. But I can't say that it is pressurized for me. It is
nothing like the tedium of appearing in court and trying to
remember what you were doing on a Friday night eighteen
months ago!

However, at the end of the six-day training period I was confident that the players understood what I was trying to achieve and
we set off to Wembley on the team coach in a positive frame of
mind. We had sorted out our tactics, and the players were up and
bubbling again, which was good to see. I knew Denmark were a
good side and I was looking forward to watching a quality match.
I felt I was finally back on the road to creating something special in
football, rather than just having a lot of hassle.

As the coach made its way down the famous Wembley Way towards the stadium, I could see the flags and feel the excitement of the fans. I hoped they would enjoy what we had to offer to them. As the team coach pulled up, I was still going over the things I needed to remind the players about, the things we'd done in training. But my main objective was to keep the dressing room very light-hearted.

The players generally keep themselves entertained by listening to music on the coach, and playing cards. Once we arrive in the dressing-room, they get changed and go out to warm up. With about twenty minutes to go the atmosphere changes and they start putting an edge on it, geeing each other up, shouting and getting ready to go out and play. Twelve minutes before the game starts the buzzer goes and that's the signal for final preparation and total concentration to take place. I thought Denmark would be very strong, very well organized at the back, with flair and good passing ability in midfield. I thought they would leave the two Laudrup brothers, Brian and Michael, to do most of the damage. I knew we would have to be patient. These days most international teams come at you on the break, very few come and dictate to you on your home ground. It's often a cagey business.

ENGLAND V DENMARK 9 March 1994
Wembley stadium
Attendance: 71,970
England: Seaman, Parker, Le Saux, Ince (Batty 67), Adams, Pallister, Platt, Gascoigne (Le Tissier 67), Shearer, Beardsley, Anderton
Denmark: Schmeichel, Dethlefsen, Rieper, Olsen, Kjeldbjerg, Larsen, Jensen, Vilfort (Frederikson 71), Christensen (Hogh 71), M Laudrup, B Laudrup
Result: 1–0
Scorer: Platt 17
Referee: Uilenberg (Holland)

I was very pleased with the way the game went and how the players responded to the new strategy. The fluidity on the right between Platt and Anderton was first class. Platt was like a second striker. He would take the short route through more of a central position to support Shearer in the penalty box, while Anderton went wide.

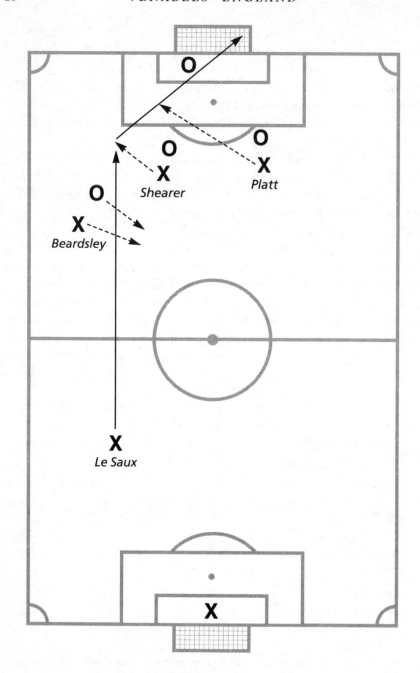

**England's goal versus Denmark**
*(scored by David Platt)*

◄----- Shows player movement        ◄——— Shows ball movement

On the left we had Gazza, and in the middle of midfield we had Ince, who was in the holding position. Ince was supporting everything and making a screen in front of the back four, and eventually I wanted to get a central defender further forward. In that case Ince would drop back to cover. However, essentially Ince had to support the ball and if he saw the opposition trying to break he should try and get into them.

Gazza doesn't naturally go wide like Anderton, so Beardsley was going wide while Gazza was taking the short route into the box. Considering that Gazza wasn't fully fit as he'd picked up an injury the previous Sunday in Italy, he played well. He missed a couple of good chances, but overall he made a good contribution. I really thought we could have had two or three goals from the match.

The goal that Platt scored was in fact a great example of what I was trying to get the team to do, and it proved how successful the training sessions had been. Le Saux had the ball, and Beardsley, who was in line to receive it, drew their right-back away, keeping him close to him and pulling him away to leave someone else free to receive the ball. Le Saux spotted this and passed the ball down the wing for Shearer to run on to. So Beardsley created space for Shearer. Platt got into the box, Shearer passed to Platt and he knocked the ball into the far side of the net. That summed up everything I wanted from my team. It is all about shifting people out of spaces and getting players into those spaces that have been left by other players.

What I normally do during the game is make two or three major points at half-time if I think it will make a difference to our game and the way we are playing. So during the first half I write bullet points down, and maybe I'll have ten written down, then I'll ask whoever I'm sitting with, that's usually the doctor, to tell me when it is five minutes to go before half-time. I will then whittle the ten points down to two or three, maximum of four, to make sure I don't overload the players with information.

Once we are back in the dressing-room, I'll let the players settle down and do whatever they have to, then I'll sit them down and make the major points, keeping things as simple as possible. Then I'll probably go round and have a word individually. It may be that four points affect four different players, so I'll go round and remind the four of each point, so they've each got one thing to remember.

It's rather like putting putty on the windscreen, you can put it all on at once and it doesn't stick, or you can put it on a bit at a time and it will gradually stick. I drip-feed them information.

I only made a couple of points at half-time during the England v Denmark match and those were concerned with getting a better balance between the three players in midfield, Anderton, Ince and Gazza, and Platt and Beardsley who were the link in scoring goals. When the ball went wide, we needed to get more players in the box to support Shearer.

After the match is a very flat time for me. The players are still talking about the game, and going over all the things that have happened, but it's not the time to sit them down and talk about the game. They're running around, one's in the shower, another's in the bath-tub. It would be a false way of conveying information, and I don't like forcing anything that's false. I did talk to the Dane John Jensen after this game and he said that Beardsley and Platt caused them a lot of problems by drawing the Danish players into areas they didn't want to go into. For example, if he picked Platt up he would go deep and Anderton would run past him and be a danger to the Danes. This meant we were asking questions of the defenders all the time and this is what I wanted to achieve, so I was very pleased to hear that from Jensen.

Anyway, it's not long before David Davies will be in to say that the television needs me. Then the radio guys want me. So I set off and go through the plunge-pool area and through the area by the showers, which is usually an inch deep in water! Then I pop out through a door behind which the television stations wait. I do the BBC and Sky interviews and then walk across the corridor to where the coaches are parked to do the radio interviews. Then I try and get the players to come and talk to the media. This depends on who's left, as they are pretty quick to go upstairs and join their families and friends in the players' lounge. Before they slip away I usually get round to most of the players just to say, 'Well done.' It's no more than that.

At club level I would sit down with them the day after the game and discuss it in more depth. I don't have the chance to do that as England Coach, so we go through it all the next time we meet. However, this is a problem as usually due to injury or other things, you don't have the same players in the next squad, so there isn't really much feedback from match to match. It's a bit like being Rent-a-Coach with Rent-a-Team, you just go out do the job, then disappear back home and get on with life. I miss the feedback and discussion sessions which you can have at club level and I think it is a distinct disadvantage not to know your players in any great depth. It's like when you were young and someone special came to your house. Out would come the best china teaset which would then be put away for another six weeks when they left.

After all this, I go and talk to what are known as the number two journalists. These are the back-up reporters, the ones who are doing follow-up stories for the next morning, while their number ones are putting over the match report to their papers. I get a barrage of questions from them. They make Jeremy Paxman look like a spokesperson for the local branch of the Women's Institute!

Then I go back to the press box, to where the number ones are still putting over copy, and I have to talk to them. It is now about eleven-fifteen, and the number ones cross-examine me for an angle to use on Friday. After another round with the written press, it's close to midnight before I start doing the interviews for the Sunday papers. This was one of the first things I changed: Bobby Robson and Graham Taylor used to meet the Press again the next day. But I found you'd go through all the same things the following day, so I said I was quite happy to go through the night doing it, but I didn't see the point in meeting up the next day. They say that they need a 'thinking piece', but they've seen the game, they've heard what I've got to say, surely it is now up to them to think?

Finally, when everyone has exhausted all the possible angles of discussion I'll meet my family for a drink before I go home. Once I'm home I will often watch the game on video. I normally don't go to sleep until three or three-thirty in the morning. I'm still very involved in the game, going through all the moves. I don't sleep-in the next day, instead I will get up and usually watch the game again. (I will often watch it again at the weekend.)

Sometimes BBC or Sky will give me a recording as seen from behind the goals, which I prefer. Last year I went to Blackburn Rovers and, as their stand was being rebuilt, the directors' box was behind the goal; and I must say I like that view. You can see right through the team, and see it move sideways and lengthways. You can also see the space between defenders and between the goalkeeper and the back four. If you're looking sideways and concentrating on the attack you can't see right through the team, whereas looking at it straight on you can look at the attack and still see what the rest are doing.

I felt that we had learnt some valuable lessons from the first match, summarized as follows:

    1. The players demonstrated that they could absorb new ideas fairly quickly and apply them efficiently on the pitch.

    2. The players have open minds.

    3. In spite of the short time we spend together we can make a lot of progress.

    4. Tactically speaking, I couldn't rely on too many specialist players in a squad due to the restriction of numbers that was likely to be imposed for Euro 96.

So, with the first match under my belt, I began to look forward to more and to experimenting with a few tactical changes to discover the final format for the European Championship finals in the summer of 1996.

# CHAPTER THREE

## THE ORGANIZATION OF THE EUROPEAN CHAMPIONSHIP

My job is to get the England team ready for the European Championship finals which will take place in England during the summer of 1996. But there is a lot more to life than that. The European Championship won't just happen, someone has to make sure that we have an infrastructure that is modern and efficient and able to take on the influx of teams, fans and tourists that such a major tournament will attract. And that person is Glen Kirton, director of Euro 96.

Glen is an old hand in the world of football. He has spent twenty-three years at the FA in various roles from press officer to commercial manager and then head of external affairs. So he was the ideal candidate to take on the awesome task of pulling everything together from an organizational point of view.

Shortly after my appointment as England Coach I met Glen at White's Hotel, near the FA headquarters. We frequently use this elegant and stylish hotel for visitors and for meetings. Glen and I had breakfast and went over the organization of the Championships. It was a very revealing meeting, and useful for me as I got to understand how difficult it is to organize a major tournament.

The European Championship has quite a chequered history. It was the dream of Henri Delaunay who, back in 1927, was the General Secretary of the French Federation. Initially, priority was given to the creation of the World Cup, and Henri had to wait until the European Federation, UEFA, was created in 1954, before he got another shot at putting the European Championship together. He was in an ideal position as he was General Secretary of UEFA, but unfortunately, he died before the launch of the Championship in 1958. However, the trophy for which up to sixteen nations compete every four years bears his name and is called the Henri Delaunay Trophy.

The European Championship continues to be run by UEFA. Initially UEFA encompassed 25 national federations but it has now risen to a record 49, due to the political changes in Eastern Europe. The current President of UEFA is Lennart Johansson of Sweden and the General Secretary is Gerhard Aigner. England is in effect just the local organizing committee for the Championship finals, and this causes some conflict between UEFA's interests and the interests of the FA and English football in general. Glen explains the situation further:

'The biggest challenge has been in organizing the commercial contracts with everyone. We have asked all the stadiums involved in hosting a match to give us all their facilities for the duration of the finals, plus all their staff, but we are not actually giving much in return. The clubs involved – Manchester United, Liverpool, Sheffield Wednesday, Leeds, Newcastle, Aston Villa and Nottingham Forest – are all being very co-operative, as they understand there is enormous prestige in being able to say that they were hosts of Euro 96 matches. But they do have their own commercial needs to consider, and it is hard to say to them, 'Well, you've invested twenty-seven million pounds in your executive boxes, but you can't have them because we want them. We'll give you ten per cent of the gate receipts, which if you're lucky – if the game is a sell-out – will amount to only about £200,000!

'Another problem relates to the club shops. UEFA, who hold all commercial rights to the tournament, have sold the rights on to a company called ISL Marketing, which is based in Switzerland. ISL in turn, have sold rights to various companies who are major sponsors, like Mars and Coca-Cola. This leaves very little money for the host country and means that all sorts of club rights are suspended for the length of the tournament. In the case of merchandising ISL have sold exclusive rights to Time Warner. In theory this means that Manchester United's shop has to close down as Time Warner have the exclusive rights to sell their products in and around the grounds. In practice, it isn't quite as bad as that: I'm sure the parties involved will find a compromise and Manchester United or Liverpool or any of the other clubs involved will produce some joint merchandise, like a Man United/Euro 96 scarf.

'The clubs involved in hosting matches have organized themselves into a small committee so that the external forces like ISL and their major sponsors can negotiate with one body instead of having to deal with each club separately. Wembley is also involved and, as it is a separate entity from the clubs, there are other problems to sort out on the commercial front with them. You can't, for example, have an on-pitch advertiser that conflicts with one of the major sponsors.

'UEFA are well aware of these problems and they will be ironed out within the next couple of years, but meanwhile we have to deal with them for the 1996 tournament. And just to make matters worse, we are experiencing the backlash from USA 94, where the local organizing committee, i.e. the Americans, organized their own official suppliers and sponsors so well that they irritated ISL's major sponsors, who didn't get the space and concessions that had been promised to them. ISL, on the other hand, understand that the host nation has to earn some money out of the whole thing, or it is just a lot of work and commitment for very little reward. So it is really a group of companies, each with their own commercial interests, fighting and jostling for position, which isn't the best way to organize a major tournament.'

It makes putting the team together child's play! But Glen hadn't finished explaining the complex manoeuvrings of it all.

'The FA is a public company and has to justify its expenditure. The administration budget for the tournament is running at about fourteen million pounds, and to recoup some of that UEFA allow us to keep 20 per cent of the ticket revenue, 10 per cent of the commercial contracts with ISL and 10 per cent of UEFA's television contract. If we have a 100 per cent attendance at all the games, then we will make a small profit. If we don't, then we won't, and so ISL have agreed to allow us, the FA, to appoint and earn money from our own sponsors. They have allowed us certain categories to recruit sponsors. One of these is computers, as it is vital we have a efficient, state-of-the-art communication and data system. Under the computer heading we have four separate categories: a systems integrator, a hardware supplier, a software supplier and a telecom supplier.'

So far it has taken Glen and his team two years to get to the point of deciding concessions, but he has a very small team. 'There are only about half a dozen of us at the moment, but we will grow to about a hundred staff and fifteen hundred volunteers. The volunteers will come from county associations, the clubs, and the referees' and supporters' organizations. We will also recruit from the universities, as although we are looking for people with common sense and an interest in football, above all we need people with linguistic skills, and we need drivers with skill and clean driving licences. A lot of the main areas of responsibility are covered by the FA's existing staff, who will gradually spend more time on organizing Euro 96.

'It is a great opportunity for England to put on a good show, and that is just what we will do. There will be cultural programmes put on by national and local authorities, which will aim to entertain not only the VIPs who will be visiting our country, but also the many fans and tourists. Obviously, our main aim is to make sure that the tournament is organized to a very high standard, but the cultural activities will be a very useful by-product and help promote England to the rest of the world. We are hoping that the Government will be involved at the highest level. In fact we want the Prime Minister to certainly participate in some way, although how and where has yet to be decided; David Davies is looking after government relations for Euro 96. It is a great opportunity for England to be in the shop window of Europe, and the tournament should be supported from the highest level of Government and industry.'

Glen has worked exceptionally hard to get all the commercial problems ironed out, and now he has to get down to the real nitty gritty of making sure the stadiums and the facilities are all up to scratch.

There will be enormous media interest. Glen expects that the number of journalists working at each ground will be about the same as for a World Cup which is between 1,500 and 2,000, so that means the facilities must be good to enable the journalists to work efficiently. Above all, there must be quick and easy access to information. He also expects there to be about a hundred television stations attending the event.

As we sipped our coffee and enjoyed a traditional English breakfast of scrambled eggs and bacon, the enormity of the whole thing began to sink in, especially as Glen had a few words to say to me about the performance of the England side. He thought that the fortunes of the England team during Euro 96 are vital to its success. As we move up through the quarter-finals and semi-finals it is crucial that the teams competing at that stage are attractive, so that the neutral fans will attend the matches, and we will keep interest in the tournament at a high level. If England do well it will increase interest in the country and the game. After 1966 there was a great surge of interest in football at grass roots level. If the same thing happens in 1996, we could help the youth of England to develop their skills.

I was delighted to hear this, as promoting football at grass roots level is one of my favourite subjects. I hope to see the local authorities and the Government put money into improving facilities in working class areas to give kids a chance to choose sport rather than other less healthy temptations.

Glen and I then parted to go our different ways, me to my office and him across the road to Lancaster Gate. As I walked up the stairs I thought of the great challenges that lay ahead, and once again I was disappointed that the FA hadn't organized a few more matches in the lead up to the Championship finals. If I am to prepare the team to its best, then the best way is to play against varied and talented opposition. You can't prepare a team for a major tournament by playing on a training pitch. If you don't have enough regular and well-planned games then there is a temptation to try and change your tactics too drastically in one game.

# CHAPTER FOUR

## THE GREEKS AND THE NORWEGIANS

**The Squad**
David Seaman – Arsenal
Tim Flowers – Blackburn Rovers
Warren Barton – Wimbledon
Rob Jones – Liverpool
Stuart Pearce – Nottingham Forest
Graeme Le Saux – Blackburn Rovers
Tony Adams – Arsenal
Gary Pallister (in squad for Greece only) – Manchester United
John Scales (replaced injured Pallister for Norway) – Liverpool
Steve Bould – Arsenal
Darren Anderton – Tottenham Hotspur
Paul Ince – Manchester United
Kevin Richardson – Aston Villa
Dennis Wise – Chelsea
Paul Merson – Arsenal
David Platt – Sampdoria
Ian Wright – Arsenal
Peter Beardsley – Newcastle United
Matthew Le Tissier – Southampton
Alan Shearer – Blackburn Rovers
Les Ferdinand – Queen's Park Rangers

As we gathered together to prepare for the matches against Greece and Norway, I had a positive report to give to the players. I told them I was pleased with their attitude and willingness to try out new things. There wasn't much more to say as we were already without some of the players who had played in the Denmark game.

My main objectives from these sessions were to consolidate what we had learnt and push forward using the same system we had used against Denmark.

However, nothing stays the same and I was without Gascoigne and Ince, so I had to readjust the midfield. I decided to bring in Richardson who was showing good form at Aston Villa, and Paul Merson who was shining at Arsenal. Effectively, with several new players, I had to start again. This is rather frustrating and unlike a club situation where you may have one or even two players out injured, but you are unlikely to have three or more out. Even if you did, the new players would be used to working with you anyway. This was the first time I'd worked with Richardson, Merson and Steve Bould, another addition to the squad from Arsenal.

The game against Greece was on the 17 May, with the Norwegian game scheduled just five days later. This only gave me one day to prepare before the Greek game, and then four days before the difficult game against the Norwegians.

I thought that what I needed for the match was a mix of young and experienced players. It's no good going in to international matches with all young players. You need the experience of older players mixed with the enthusiasm and potential talent of the younger ones. That is one of the reasons why I picked Beardsley. I've always been a big fan of his from the point of view of ability as well as his enthusiasm for the game. He's a very special person. He's looked after himself very well and I thought he'd been written off too soon. He's also very good with those around him. I needed intelligence.

I knew that Darren Anderton picked things up very quickly and I had found out that Le Saux was a quick learner. Those players combined with Platt, Shearer and Adams, who were all experienced internationals and good pros. Pallister was injured so I brought Steve Bould in because of his underrated ability as a defender and passer of the ball, and also because of his partnership with his Arsenal captain Adams.

ENGLAND V GREECE 17 May 1994
Wembley stadium
Attendance: 23,659
England: Flowers, Jones (Pearce 82), Le Saux, Richardson, Bould, Adams, Platt, Merson, Shearer, Beardsley (Wright 70), Anderton (Le Tissier 62)
Greece: Karkamanis, Apostolakis, Karayannis, Kolitsidakis, (Karataidis 45), Kalitzakis, Tsalouchidis, Hantzidis (Mitropoulos 45), Nioplias, Mahlas (Nikos 45), Savvas (Kostis 69), Tsiantakis
Result: 5–0
Scorers: Anderton 24, Beardsley 37, Platt 45 (pen) 55, Shearer 65
Referee: J McCluskey (Scotland)

In the light of the fact that we won 5–0 against the Greeks, most people have written them off as not very strong competition, but that is rubbish. There is no such thing as an easy option. You have to remember that Greece had been first to qualify for the World Cup finals, finishing above Russia in their group. They certainly merited respect and the right to be taken seriously. Although they didn't have a very good World Cup they were, in May 1994, top of their qualifying group for the European Championship finals.

Bould and Richardson were the two new caps, and along with Paul Merson, who hadn't played for a long while, performed particularly well. When it comes down to picking a squad I have to rely on my football intuition as well as the more tangible reports that my scouts prepare on the players. I thought Richardson was a very influential player who had the experience and the personality to slot straight in, and he did that. After this game Richardson didn't put in the same performances with his club and when that happens and the player is older, you are uncertain whether he is temporarily dipping in form or whether age is catching up with him. When you don't know a player that well, you have to judge him on what you see. I think Richardson was unlucky not to go on from there, but I had to go on his form, which wasn't that good the following season. Merson's form dipped after this match too, and, of course, we knew why when his problems came to light later.

I have had a bit of a dilemma about Bould as I think he is an excellent player and a lot better passer than he has been credited with. He plays well with Adams and I rate Bould highly. I had to try and get one of the centre-halves to come forward, but both Adams and Bould are quite set in their ways; they don't like to venture forward. I did think that with encouragement they would have been able to do that, but in the end I stuck with Adams as my first-choice player.

Shearer had a really excellent game. After this match everyone was saying he must be one of the best players in Europe. He pulled them around, he scored, he did just about everything. I was delighted that Darren Anderton scored in only his second match. Anderton and Graeme Le Saux looked like they had been playing for England for years.

David Platt scored two goals that took his exceptional tally up to 23 strikes in 47 games which is almost a goal every other match. David is one of those players who, through his intelligence, has made the best out of all his talents. In addition to this, he has a very steady head, which makes him a good captain. He has done everything and has the experience to command respect from the older players. Tony Adams is also absolutely outstanding as a captain. He has great leadership qualities and a unique and highly successful way of transferring what he thinks to the players. He is always talking to them and telling them what he wants from them and how they can improve. He also has tact and diplomacy. He has played a vital part in Arsenal winning six trophies in the last few years. Adams was the captain who lifted up the cups and this experience is important for England. It is difficult to make a choice between these two.

I decided on the same tactics for the game against Greece as I had used against Denmark. It paid off. We didn't start very confidently, but the main thing was we recovered quickly, took control of the game, and scored five times. It was disappointing to see Wembley only a third full, but I thought a lot of fans would be wanting to come to see Norway five days later.

We played in our wine red away strip. I wasn't too pleased about this. It was explained to me that as we didn't have any away matches planned, it was an ideal chance to present it to the general public.

ENGLAND V NORWAY 22 May 1994
Wembley stadium
Attendance: 64,327
England: Seaman, Jones, Le Saux, Ince (Le Tissier 76), Bould,
Adams, Platt, Wise, Shearer, Beardsley, Anderton (Wright 76)
Norway: Thorstvedt (By Rise 87), H Berg, Johnsen, Bratseth,
Nilsen (Haåland 45), Flo, O Berg (Ingebrigtsen 67), Bohinen,
Fjørtoft (Sorloth 45), Rekdal, Jakobsen
Result: 0–0
Referee: K Nielsen (Denmark)

I knew that this would be a much tougher test. There was a
score to settle: Norway had beaten us on the way to the World
Cup.

Personally, I wanted the Norway game before the Greek fix-
ture. I knew that there would be quite a bit of hanging around in
the four days between the games, and I though this could work to
our disadvantage. To combat the boredom I have implemented a
series of talks from other professionals. One we have planned is a
chat with the police on hooliganism. I think this will be good for
the players because we are often irritated when the game is held up
by crowd trouble. If we understand the implications of what is
going on, then it makes us more patient and aware of the difficul-
ties that could be going on around the pitch. We were also at the
end of the season and many of the players were tired after a heavy
year playing in the Premier League. The players will have a 10-day
rest before they come to me for the European Championship
finals.

We did well against Norway, despite the result. Shearer scored,
but the referee disallowed it. I knew that the system I had installed
in the team would work well for us and cause problems for
Denmark and Greece but I also knew it wouldn't be the same
against Norway because of the way they play, which is very defensively, with most of the team in their half. However, I wanted to
continue the way we had started, so that when the players broke
for summer they would have something consistent to think about.

This period had also been a learning curve for me, and I
wanted to go away and consider what we had achieved and what
still needed working on.

Against Denmark and Greece, I had managed to lengthen and

stretch the opposition on the right in both games with Anderton, and on the left with Beardsley and Merson respectively. However, things were a little different with Norway.

Norway play their back four within the width of the box (see over), and then they play the midfield with no space in front of them. If they squeeze up or drop off, the space is so small that our players don't have a chance to get through. If Platt goes to one side he has to go through the whole team, and if we knock the ball over the top, then they will squeeze up for offside.

Normally the players marking Platt would come out with him, but these guys stay put. They are happy to let you go back as you've still got to break through them. You can't pass across the box as they have the width covered. What they do is try and catch you out on the break, or pass long balls through to the big striker who can flick the ball on.

You have to be careful as they will hit you with long balls and fast support. As soon as they lose the ball, they revert back to their original positions. That's why playing against Norway is always such a boring game. Norway's big mistake is that having made strides with this quite clever negative way of playing, they didn't make an effort to improve. Tactically speaking you can't stand still in football because you end up going backwards as other nations overtake you, and that's what has happened to Norway.

If Egil Olsen, the Norwegian coach, could have created a clever attacking game to go hand in hand with their defensive game, then they would have made progress. They have players who are strong, big and fit, and so their system has worked up until now. They knocked England out of the World Cup, but when they came up against top opposition they lost. They haven't qualified for Euro 96, so maybe they will be forced to change their style and think to the future.

Summing things up after the first three matches, I was pleased with the way things were going. The few new players I'd brought in were adjusting in a mature fashion to the demands put on them and the tactical changes I'd brought in had worked well. The players had adapted in a very short time, and that made me particularly optimistic about the future.

Graham Taylor was criticized for making radical changes to the team in two previous matches against Norway. Things went as they did and you can't change that, the only thing is to look

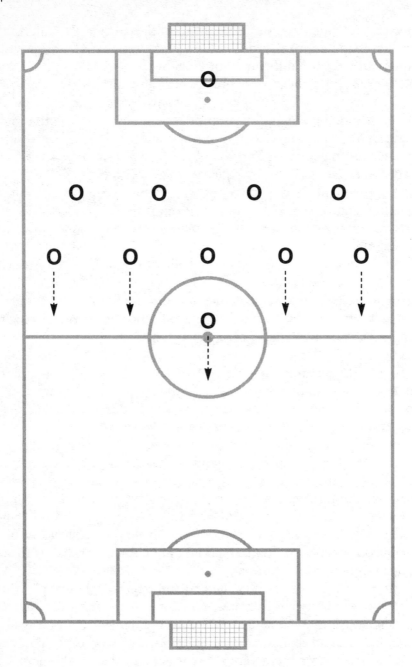

**Norway's formation showing defensive football
– moving forward to attack**

◄---- Shows player movement

forward. My methods are different, I want to bring change in slowly and gradually develop the kind of play that I want for the European Championship. I wanted to do three things in the following order:-

1. Set out a system.
2. Tell the players what I wanted from them.
3. Show them how to do it.

I wasn't so concerned with details. In my mind I wanted to have a fair idea of the players I wanted for my squad by Christmas 1995, and from January 1996 onwards I would be working on fine-tuning the tactics and other details like set pieces, which I want to leave to last so our opponents will have a few surprises thrown at them. But to be fair to Graham I have the luxury of having to play only in friendly matches, and so I can have a longer period in which to adjust the team. This is the other side of the coin of not playing in competitive games.

As far as the team was concerned, after these matches we were all feeling a lot better about ourselves. The psychological state of the team was as important to me as the actual results. I was pretty sure that once our confidence was back everything else would fall into place. I also wanted other countries to start being afraid of us again. I think that was beginning to happen.

So as I set off to the World Cup in America I was feeling good about the future and travelled with the objective of seeing some good games and learning about the teams who could be our eventual opponents.

# CHAPTER FIVE

## THE WORLD CUP

The World Cup is the pinnacle of what we managers set out to achieve. There can be no greater moment of glory than seeing your team lifting the World Cup trophy. It is the accumulation of years of experience, combined with the ability to pick the right players and a large amount of luck to ensure that your best players don't get injured before or during the event. As always, I was very excited about being involved with the World Cup, even if it was on the sidelines.

I worked for the BBC as an analyst. My job was to offer an informed opinion about as many of the games as possible. The first thing for me to decide was when I was going out to the United States, and which matches I was going to see. America is such a large place that it was not going to be physically possible to be there and catch all the games I would like to see. So I decided to stay at home for the first two weeks and watch the initial part of the tournament in the studios. Some people say that you can see it better on television, but I think that videos are exceptionally beneficial because you can play them again and again and study the various points of the game.

When you are at the game, you can get a view of the bigger picture, but you either see the action as it happens or, unless you're videoing it at home, you only see it once. I feel that the growth of the video has made us somewhat lazy and less willing to concentrate. Before videos, you really had to focus on the game as it happened.

I went to the BBC studios in the morning and was often still there to watch the evening games. It was a great opportunity to catch three or four matches a day, which you could never do if you were actually in America watching live.

As the competition thinned out to the quarter- and semi-finals, I went out to America and watched Brazil v Holland in Dallas, then Germany v Bulgaria and Italy v Bulgaria in the Giants Stadium in New Jersey. This must be the most magnificent sporting stadium in the world. It smells of sport as you come up to the pitch from underneath it. The dressing-room areas are underground and as you walk out into the open air it feels as if the whole stadium is wrapped around you; it is quite awe-inspiring. I never got tired of this incredible sight.

Of course there are a lot of stadiums that are getting better and better as more improvements take place. And a lot of our stadiums are going to be very impressive for the European Championship finals.

I thought the World Cup as a whole was the best I have ever seen. I'm not saying that there weren't better individual matches in other World Cups, but across the board the quality was kept consistently high. I kept thinking that I was bound to be disappointed by the next game, but I wasn't. Virtually every game had goals, invention, great finishing and great entertainment. It was organized very well: the marriage of the game and the organization was second to none in America.

I think there are several explanations for this. One of the most important steps forward has been the technical changes, particularly the ban on tackling from behind. It gives the advantage back to the creative player, which is to the good of the game, and it also gives us five or six extra minutes of play. The ball was in play for that much longer because the players were able to turn and play football in areas they hadn't been able to play in before, and there was less time taken for injuries.

The rule that allowed tackling from behind gave advantage to the defender, now the advantage has passed back to the attacking player, and the defender has to be more skilful. It has stopped defenders from just crashing in, instead they have to solve the problem of getting the ball.

But just to linger on some of the technical points of the World Cup: Holland started off their 3–2 quarter-final defeat against Brazil quite defensively and were then on the wrong end of the new rule which now states that you can't be offside in a non-active zone. When, rather naively, they left Brazil offside in this situation, twice the eventual winners were awarded the goals.

Once they were 2–0 down, Holland started playing an attacking game, and it became very entertaining. The Dutch pulled one back through Dennis Bergkamp and then equalized through Aron Winter. It made me wonder what would have happened if Holland had gone out on to the pitch with a more aggressive, attacking attitude from the kick-off. But they were effectively finished when the Brazilian Branco scored a hell of a goal from a 30-yard free-kick.

I really thought that Holland were one of the unluckiest teams to go out of the World Cup in the way they did. They had the skill and technique to beat the Brazilians, if only they had begun in top gear.

After that I went to see Germany v Bulgaria, and I have to say that I fancied Bulgaria. Germany were quite an old team, a lot of players were coming to the twilight years of their careers. True to my initial thoughts, after a good start the age difference started to show.

Klinsmann went down for a penalty and scored. Then Bulgaria equalized through a Stoichkov free-kick, and eventually Lechkov headed in off the back post to win the game. It was a great result. Bulgaria had some talented individual players like Balakov, Kostadinov, Sirakov and Lechkov, and they played exceptionally well.

One of the great things about the Italy – Bulgaria semi-final was the atmosphere. There were so many Italian fans in and around New York their presence added a great carnival-like atmosphere to the game. Of course, the really outstanding performance was from Roberto Baggio. He was just on fire for twenty minutes. It was electrifying. Every time he brought the ball, it brought you to the edge of your seat wondering what he could possibly do next. He was essentially the difference between the two teams, and the reason that Italy went through.

And that brought us to the final between Brazil and Italy. Over the years, these two teams have given us some great matches. When they met in the 1982 World Cup finals the match was considered to be one of the great classics, and Italy having won, then went on to win the final, and take their third World Cup title.

Paolo Rossi, who came back into the game after a two-year ban for allegedly being involved in a 'fixing' scandal, reached the pinnacle of his career by scoring six goals in three matches. He scored a hat-trick in the match against the Brazilians, which the Italians won 3–2. But it wasn't just Rossi who was on form. There was the marvellous fluidity from midfield genius Marco Tardelli and a solid defence headed by Antonio Cabrini and Gaetano Scirea, with a forty-year-old Dino Zoff in goal.

The World Cup final between Brazil and Italy in 1970 was another great match. This time the Brazilians won by a resounding 4–1 in a great example of attacking football. Both teams had previously won the World Cup twice, and so whoever won this match would be the permanent holders of the Jules Rimet Trophy.

As I remembered these games, I took my seat and was looking forward to another meeting between these two giants of world football. But one thing that was going through my mind was whether football had changed so much over the years that we could ask ourselves: Have tactics caught talent up? To some extent tactics can eliminate talent, but the really outstanding talent will always tip the balance. A good example of this was Roberto Baggio in the semi-final against Bulgaria. Baggio was simply outstanding and impossible for the Bulgarians to deal with, so he changed the balance of the game in Italy's favour. Either of them could have gone through to the final, but Italy just had the edge.

As there were no goals and the game was decided on penalties, a lot of people have said that it was a disappointing match. But I've watched it since, and it was a really good game. It was good-quality football, produced by two outstanding sides. I thought there was a gap between Brazil and Italy, which wasn't really shown during the game. Having watched it again on video I feel that Brazil were the better side and deserved to win. Italy were very defensive and they were hampered by the fact that Baggio wasn't a hundred per cent fit.

I have to say that he did well to get to the final having taking quite a bashing during the semi-final. Franco Baresi did really well to get through, too. He was still recovering from a small cartilage operation and he did exceptionally well to get running, let alone manage to compete in a World Cup Final.

Baresi's tournament started slowly, but by the end he was more like the old player we were used to seeing. Overall, I think that

Romario and Bebeto were outstanding. Brazil took the risk of placing all the goal-scoring responsibility on the shoulders of these two. But I think the most influential player in the Brazilian team was Mauro da Silva. His technical ability combined with his tactical brain was amazing. He was like the coach on the pitch. He knew when to play in midfield, when to go into the defending area, and when and where support was needed. They say that he's a computer expert, and he obviously has that type of brain. He consistently knew what position to be in right through the tournament – he must have fitted a computer inside his head.

I was delighted that Brazil won. It was a majestic end to a magnificent competition. Playing against a side like Brazil is the ultimate yardstick.

There are a couple of points I'd like to make about the World Cup. First, although the tournament as run by FIFA has worked well, I do believe that the World Union of Players and Coaches should have a say in certain matters. The players certainly wouldn't have voted to play the World Cup Final in Los Angeles at midday in over 100°F of heat.

This was obviously done for television, but quite frankly, something as important as a World Cup Final deserves more respect. It was so important that it would be watched at any time of the day, as a Grand Prix is when it takes place in Japan or Australia. Even New York would have been more advantageous from the point of view of timing. To play such an important match in adverse weather conditions is denigrating the game.

The other point I wish to make concerns penalties. Out of the forty-eight penalties taken in the World Cup, not one was retaken even though in at least half of them the goalkeeper moved before the penalty taker kicked the ball. This is a very difficult decision for the referee to make. If he makes the player retake the penalty, who is he penalising? I think it would be much easier if the goalkeeper was allowed to move and the penalty taker was allowed to stop on his run-up to the ball. This would result in self-regulation as the goalkeeper wouldn't move if he thought the player could stop.

I flew back to London with my head brimming with ideas on how I needed to adjust my tactics to produce a team that could take on the best and win. I know it will be a slow, careful progressive path towards the European Championship finals, but the important thing is that we make progress. It is obvious that the flat, square way of playing is not only old-fashioned, but plays into opposition hands. I have to have more fluidity in midfield, so that when we are playing a team like Portugal who have a packed midfield, we can meet them in terms of numbers and strength. That means full-backs must, when required, push forward and close the space between the defence and the midfield. It also means adjusting the positions of the two strikers; so one is slightly deeper, causing problems to the opposition's defence. I pulled out my pen and started scribbling tactics.

# CHAPTER SIX

## THE USA, ROMANIA AND NIGERIA

**England v USA**
**The Squad**
David Seaman – Arsenal
Tim Flowers – Blackburn Rovers
Rob Jones – Liverpool
Tony Adams – Arsenal
Gary Pallister – Manchester United
Barry Venison – Newcastle United
Graeme Le Saux – Blackburn Rovers
Stuart Pearce – Nottingham Forest
Darren Anderton –Tottenham Hotspur
Robert Lee – Newcastle United
David Platt – Sampdoria
Matthew Le Tissier – Southampton
Dennis Wise – Chelsea
Neil Ruddock – Liverpool
Les Ferdinand – Queen's Park Rangers
Ian Wright – Arsenal
Alan Shearer – Blackburn Rovers
Teddy Sheringham – Tottenham Hotspur
John Barnes – Liverpool

I thought it would be nice to get a couple of teams from the World Cup to Wembley and the USA had definitely done better than expected and have continued to do so. They were finally knocked out of the tournament on Independence Day, 4 July, 1994, by the eventual winners, Brazil. They felt good after this and I thought it would be an extremely useful game for us as the USA are still something of an unknown quantity.

ENGLAND V USA 7 September 1994
Wembley stadium
Attendance: 38,629
England: Seaman, Jones, Le Saux, Venison, Adams, Pallister, Platt, Barnes, Shearer (Ferdinand 80), Sheringham (Wright 80), Anderton
USA: Friedel (Sommer 82), Caligiuri, Lalas, Balboa, Agoos, (Lapper 70), Perez (Wynalda 45), Dooley, Reyna (Moore 82), Sorber, Jones, Stewart (Klopas 82)
Result: 2–0
Scorer: Shearer 32, 39
Referee: A Lopez Nieto (Spain)

We ended up winning it well, 2–0, and it could have been more. The black spot was the behaviour of some of our fans during the national anthems. A certain section of the fans, mostly young kids, booed and jeered. It was an embarrassment to all of us. We had been concerned about the booing since the first match against Denmark, but at the USA game it had reached a level where it simply wasn't acceptable any more. It also gave their players an unnecessary psychological advantage, as the England players felt embarrassed by the behaviour of some of their own fans.

After the game David Davies started a campaign through the Press to stop that kind of behaviour. David had lunch with some of the sports editors of the national newspapers, who agreed to put over the fact that by booing the opposition's national anthem, the fans were giving an advantage to the opposition's players by winding them up. And it worked, the fans have been much better behaved since.

But back to the technicalities of the match. I had been happy with the Christmas tree formation, but I decided to change it slightly and implement the system that had worked so well for me at Barcelona. This meant having two players up front that would play up front but would try and come in off the opposition's full-backs rather than the centre-halves. This would effectively make the centre-halves redundant, and if there is one thing a centre-half

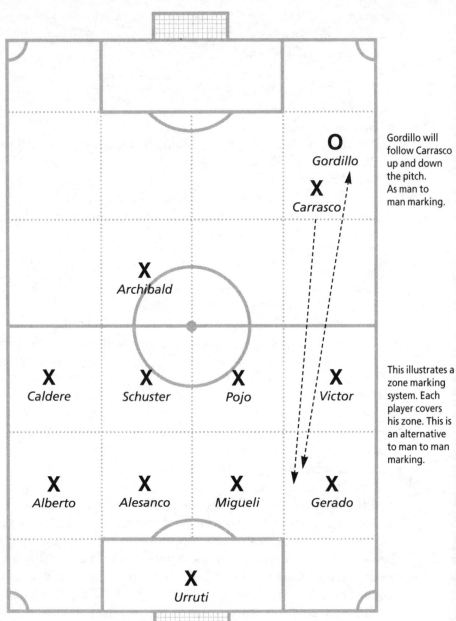

**Zone Marking System with Barcelona**
*devised by Terry Venables*

◄---- Shows player movement

hates more than anything else it is being unsure about who to mark. Basically, I put two defensive players out on the wing in midfield so they could drop back and squeeze up the defence. At Barcelona I put Schuster and Rocco, my two attacking players, in the middle of the field, which is unusual. This meant that Rocco could go wide. Translated into the present England team, Platt, Barmby or McManaman, can come through using the wings as well as coming through the middle. I also used this system with QPR. They won the second division title with this and we went up to the first division and qualified for Europe at the first go. I wanted goalscorers and wide players from movement not from players who were already in position. I wanted three wide players, and if one went wide the other two would get into the box to receive the cross.

I tried to do the same thing at Barcelona, with Steve Archibald, who was a wonderful player, and unlike at QPR, I put my defensive players out on the wing so they could, if necessary come back to defend, which enabled the full-backs to come in narrow. This gave us six defending players and the attacking players in central midfield, which effectively gave me four attacking players. This made it very difficult for the opposition to come forward and enabled the back four to get very close and not leave any spaces. It was a very mobile system, which meant that the players could react and move according to how the game was going. I was able to create space and this is very important. I couldn't use this system at Tottenham when I first arrived, as I simply didn't have the players who could play to it.

In the USA match, Platt played in the 'hole' i.e. in the space behind the front two players. His job was to get into the box and go wide as well. My instructions to them were that if one of the three players – Shearer, Sheringham or Platt – went wide, the other two had to get in the box for the cross. David Platt is very adaptable as he can score vital goals and act as another striker.

Shearer and Le Saux worked very well together during the game. Shearer got the two goals but Le Saux did a lot of work as well. They seem to have a natural ability to communicate and know what each other is doing, and it obviously helps that they play together at Blackburn. Their reactions to each other are instinctive. For example, Le Saux hardly has to lift his head to know exactly where Shearer will be.

Other national teams have built their sides around the natural advantage of players playing together in the same club team. Ajax players form most of the Dutch team, and in 1982, when Italy won the World Cup for the third time, the backbone of their team consisted of Juventus players. The goalkeeper, Dino Zoff, defender Antonio Cabrini, sweeper Gaetano Scirea, midfielder Marco Tardelli and striker Paolo Rossi, all played for Juventus.

The advantage of having players who already know and work with each other is enormous, but it is very difficult to do this with England. There is one insurmountable problem, and that is nationality. Ron Greenwood tried to do this by picking five or six Liverpool players, but some of the best Liverpool players are Irishmen, Scotsmen or Welshmen, and that is the problem. We are not one nation, but four, and there tend to be a higher proportion of 'foreigners' in club teams. I know the same can be said for foreign clubs who buy world-class foreign stars, and it is often the case that national teams from countries who have a high percentage of foreigners playing for their clubs find their form dipping and consistency harder to achieve.

Sheringham also had a good game and I was beginning to form the opinion that he, Le Saux and Shearer would be my first choice for the 1995 summer tournament.

I was criticized for giving a new cap to Barry Venison, but he played well and silenced the critics. He held the middle of the park very effectively. He filled in positions and I knew that if I allowed the centre-half freedom to break and make an extra player go forward he would always fill in. Venison is an intelligent player and very rarely gave the ball away. In fact he passed the ball to a team-mate very quickly, which maximized the space he had.

Barnes was on the left, with Anderton on the right. They were both workers who could manipulate the ball well, and I felt we gave the Americans a hard time in trying to get the ball away from us.

The Americans were on a $25,000 bonus to win the game. On reflection it was probably a bit soon after the World Cup, and they may have been feeling somewhat de-motivated. It's difficult to get the players going again after a major tournament, as the adrenalin's gone. The Americans started well but then tailed off.

Before the match, we had a minute's silence for Billy Wright, who had died the previous weekend. He was a wonderful England player, who got over 100 caps and, along with Bobby Moore, was one of our all-time greats.

I was pleased with the way we played and how quickly the players had picked up a different system. We went away from the game with our record of not conceding any goals still intact. We hadn't lost any games either, and I felt we were building a strong platform from which to tackle the most demanding matches. One of the most important aspects was that I was getting to know my team and which players adjusted well to being in the England shirt and which ones wouldn't make the grade.

### England v Romania
### The Squad
David Seaman – Arsenal
Tim Flowers – Blackburn Rovers
Rob Jones – Liverpool
Tony Adams – Arsenal
Gary Pallister – Manchester United
Neil Ruddock – Liverpool
Graeme Le Saux – Blackburn Rovers
Stuart Pearce – Nottingham Forest
Steve McManaman – Liverpool
Robert Lee – Newcastle United
Matthew Le Tissier – Southampton
Paul Ince – Manchester United
Dennis Wise – Chelsea
John Barnes – Liverpool
Les Ferdinand – Queen's Park Rangers
Ian Wright – Arsenal
Alan Shearer – Blackburn Rovers
Teddy Sheringham – Tottenham Hotspur

It was a blow that both Anderton and Beardsley were injured as they had been doing well. However, I thought this would give me the chance to look at Ian Wright and Matt Le Tissier.

I knew that Romania were very good at bringing their full-backs forward, so we had to get Wright and Le Tissier wide. This wasn't their natural game, but I wanted to see if they could adapt to this. I was also thinking of playing the same system as I played against the USA, but with Wright and Shearer up front instead of

Shearer and Sheringham, with Le Tissier playing behind them rather than Platt.

As well as wide full-backs, Romania also had two wide wingers and my main concern was that we would be too narrow to deal with it. I decided therefore to play Wright and Le Tissier wide.

I knew that Wright had played that way for Arsenal, especially in European matches, and Le Tissier had also played in a wide position for his club. I thought the players responded well to the changes, and it was an experiment that I was prepared to gamble on.

ENGLAND V ROMANIA 12 October 1994
Wembley stadium
Attendance: 48,754
England: Seaman, Jones (Pearce 59), Le Saux, Ince, Adams, Pallister, Lee (Wise 71), Wright (Sheringham 71), Shearer, Barnes, Le Tissier
Romania: Stelea (Prunea 87), Petrescu, Prodan, Belodedici, Lupescu, Popescu, Lacatus (Cirstea 81), Dumitrescu, Raducioiu (Timofte 77), Hagi (Selymes 45), Munteanu
Result 1–1
Scorers: Dumitrescu 37, Lee 45
Referee: J Quiniou (France)

I thought Romania were very good opposition. Their players started the game particularly well. They demonstrated very good ball control, but didn't make a lot of progress. We should have stopped their goal, but there was a hesitation in our defence which allowed them to score. Up until that point Adams and Pallister had looked like two centre-halves who wouldn't give many goals away. Dumitrescu took it very well, but we kept at it and equalized and, quite frankly, we should have won the game.

Unfortunately, there wasn't enough support from midfield, or from the wide players, for Shearer. I wasn't happy with the way we dealt tactically with Romania, and I knew I'd have to work on tightening up the roles and doing more work on exactly what was expected of each player.

We got a goal back through a typical Robert Lee strike. It was a cross from Le Saux, headed down by Shearer into the path of Lee, who grabbed the chance and took it very positively.

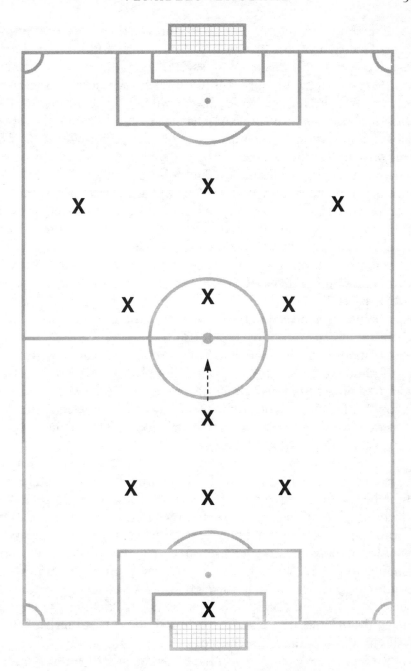

**England's formation versus Romania**

◄---- Shows player movement

There was some contention about whether Popescu should have been sent off for bringing Shearer down, and it was a shame the decision wasn't given – you wait ninety minutes to see a player like Shearer given the opportunity to pit his wits against the goal-keeper. But the referee decided otherwise. Not being involved in club football has given me the chance to stand back and look at what's going on in the game, and study the performances of various people, like the referees.

It is clear that referees are undoubtedly under pressure. The competition and rigours of life are such that in every area we are all getting very aggressive, competitive and greedy. Everyone is under pressure, but we should take stock of our own positions and, whether we are directors, managers, coaches, players, supporters or referees, ask ourselves if we are making the right decisions or just doing things because it's easier than insisting on the right moral path. I don't think we should be hammering the referees; instead we should be looking at ways of helping them, and making their job easier; alleviating the pressure so the referee can do what he is supposed to do, namely take control of the match.

I think there should be some in-built self-regulation in the game to prevent referees always having to make the decisions. For example, if someone encroaches on a ten-yard kick outside the box and they won't go back the referee has to ask himself, Do I book one player? Do I book the lot?

Another thing I would change is the referee's responsibility for timekeeping. I feel very strongly about this. If he has to take the time he then becomes constantly worried about such things as the thirty seconds he has to allow for the trainer to come on. Why should the time left to be played be a secret from everyone? Why shouldn't there be a big clock so we all know exactly how long there is to go? Someone has to be solely responsible for timekeeping. Let's see if we can help the game from a technological point of view. We talk about television replays and the ability to see things instantly through the progress of computers. Well, let's explore ways in which advanced technology can help the game.

In tennis, for example, you have sideline judges, a centre judge and a judge at the back of the court, who are all there to make the game more professional. Could we apply something similar in football? Would it be possible to use the eye of the camera for line decisions only? After an inquiry it may be found that these innovations are not applicable to our game, but we have to at least look at the possibilities.

Anyway, to sum up the Romania game, I didn't think it was as bad as everyone made out, but it was definitely not our best game. I felt we were not as good as we could have been tactically, and this made me look at myself and ask whether we would have been better keeping to the same pattern of play that we had had in the previous game. It was a good learning point for me. If the wide players had been taken back, then the inside players, Lee and Barnes, should have been able to get forward more quickly. Although Lee had been doing that for his club, Barnes is more of a manipulator of the ball, keeping control of it, rather than being a forward running-player.

### England v Nigeria
### The Squad
David Seaman – Arsenal
Tim Flowers – Blackburn Rovers
Rob Jones – Liverpool
Warren Barton – Wimbledon
Ugo Ehiogu – Aston Villa
Steve Howey – Newcastle United
Neil Ruddock – Liverpool
Graeme Le Saux – Blackburn Rovers
Stuart Pearce – Nottingham Forest
Peter Beardsley – Newcastle United
Steve McManaman – Liverpool
Robert Lee – Newcastle United
David Platt – Sampdoria
Dennis Wise – Chelsea
John Barnes – Liverpool
Matthew Le Tissier – Southampton
Teddy Sheringham – Tottenham Hotspur
Les Ferdinand – Queen's Park Rangers
Alan Shearer – Blackburn Rovers

The training camp routine was settling down well. We leave the team hotel for the training ground at 9.30am. Before that, breakfast is laid out and the players wander in as they please.

They are all different: some like to arrive early and read the papers, others like to lie in and grab a slice of toast at the last minute. Apart from the physios Alan Smith and Dave Butler, Doctor Crane and the coach driver, the earliest lark is David Platt, who arrives immaculate and alert at the breakfast table, armed with the morning's papers and ready to start another day with England. As I've already said, David is extremely responsible and I've no doubt he'll have a great career off the pitch when his playing days are over.

ENGLAND V NIGERIA 16 November 1994
Wembley stadium
Attendance: 37,196
England: Flowers, Jones, Howey, Ruddock, Le Saux, Wise, Lee (McManaman 25), Platt, Barnes, Beardsley (Le Tissier 79), Shearer (Sheringham 79)
Nigeria: Rufai, Okafor, Eguavon, Okechukwu, Iroha, George, Adepoju (Kanu 85), Okocha, Amunike, Amokachi (Ikpeba 60), Yekini (Ekoku 60)
Result: 1–0
Scorer: Platt 44, 54
Referee: L Sundell (Sweden)

What was particularly rewarding about this game was the fact that the two fresh faces who came in, Ruddock and Howey, played extremely well together. Both Adams and Pallister were out injured. Up to this point our defenders had given away very few goals, and so I needed to ensure that Howey and Ruddock were fully integrated into the team. They had already been training with us in the squad, all they had to do was carry this through to the team. Ruddock plays in a back three at Liverpool, and now he was going to play in a four with Howey (as he did for me at Tottenham), so I thought it was extremely important that we didn't do anything complicated. I wanted them to concentrate on giving shape to the back four and not risk coming forward. And they both adapted well. Howey hardly gave the ball away at all, and Ruddock was efficient with both his short and long passing.

I knew that it was important we held our own for the first fifteen or twenty minutes as I expected the Nigerians to come on very strong. And that is exactly what happened. They had a bit of a flurry, then the game settled down, and we played better and better as time went on. We won the game with a header from Platt who always scores those important goals. This one was from a well-taken free-kick by Dennis Wise. We should have gone on to win by three or four.

Dennis Wise was without doubt the best player on the night. He started off on the right and then converted to the left. He ended up contributing a lot to the overall game. Personally, I think that as well as ability, attitude and the desire to play are very important, and Dennis has loads of enthusiasm and commitment. Everyone wants to play for their country, but many of the players have the right temperament to play for England. After this match I felt I could add Wise to that list. I also thought Barnes and Beardsley sat very well alongside Wise in keeping the ball and making Nigeria run around us.

All in all I felt that my first few months as England Coach had gone according to plan. I was beginning to get to know the players and find out their capabilities on the pitch, and their personalities off it. I was discovering who were England players and which players may have the ability but weren't yet ready to make the psychological jump from club player to national team player. I was also beginning to think about involving the younger players like McManaman, Redknapp, and Barmby.

# CHAPTER SEVEN

## OFF-PITCH ACTIVITIES

As well as coaching the England team, there are many other aspects to the role of England Coach. For a start, you get involved in the game on an international basis, such as attending UEFA- and FIFA-run seminars and courses.

One of the first of these that I attended was in Sweden in September 1994. It was a general debriefing after the World Cup. Many of the coaches from the World Cup were there, including Carlos Alberto Parreira. Here are his key points on how he won the World Cup with Brazil, in America in 1994.

1. **Targets** My one and only objective was to win the World Cup. Everyone, from the football federation executives through to the Press and the fans, expected us to win the World Cup. It simply wasn't good enough to reach the final and come second. We had to win, so I made this my number one target and stuck to it.

2. **The myth** We had not had success in the last five World Cups, and so people and, more worryingly, the players, began to think we were not up to it. The gloss started to go from our bright yellow shirts. I knew from travelling around the world that people still held us in high esteem, but I had to rebuild the myth within our own environment. With this in mind, I came to Europe to speak to our players who are playing with European clubs. I told them that they had to forget about earning big bonuses and to concentrate on the honour of playing for Brazil. I told all the players that the best way to build their careers is to show what they can do with Brazil on the

world stage, which presents them with a priceless opportunity, and they all took this to heart.

3. **Style of play** The previous national coach, Lazarone, had only had one year in which to change the way the team played to meet his requirements before the Italian World Cup in 1990. It didn't work, and I decided that we had to draw on our traditional way of playing and build on this. It is no good trying to play a completely different style of football in the national team to that played at club level. I returned to playing the traditional flat back four, with a sweeper in front of them, and to use the zonal defence system, as opposed to man-to-man marking. I decided to devise a system and stick to it whoever our opposition were. I was lucky in that Dunga quickly established himself as did Mauro da Silva.

My biggest challenge as a coach was to organize the players when they didn't have the ball. The players who play in Italy understand the importance of being 100 per cent organized in closing down and marking the opposition. A team has to attack with ten players. It's OK to be creative when you have the ball, but you have to learn to be disciplined and organized without it.

4. **Impose the Brazilian style on the game** This meant sticking to a system and never changing it.

5. **The need to win off the pitch** The team organization and harmony was a disaster in Italy in 1990. I knew that I had to ensure that everything was efficient off the pitch, so we could just concentrate on playing. In Italy, there was the problem of the wives and girlfriends. On the morning of one match, a player rang the coach to say that his wife and child had just arrived at the airport and they didn't have a hire car or any transport to get them to the hotel and then on to the match. This was crazy, the player should have been concentrating on the match.

From the beginning, I stipulated that the wives and families could come, but they could not stay with the players, and in addition to this there would be no specially allocated time for them to meet. I instructed the organizers to erect a tent about 20 metres from our hotel, and this was to be used to receive visitors, including families. No one outside of the authorized personnel was allowed into the team hotel. On their free days the players could meet people in this tented area, including their club managers, who at the last World Cup were trying to discuss contracts in the team hotel! This rule made us very united as a team. We had very little time to prepare for the qualification matches, and we had to cope with varying altitudes, such as in Bolivia, which is 4,000 metres above sea level. But this time spent together paid off. When we got to America the players linked hands to walk on to the pitch, and this show of unity stayed with us throughout the tournament.

6. **Pre-World Cup preparation** We only had one month in which to prepare for the World Cup finals. In 1970, the team had three and a half months. In 1974 and 1978 two months. In 1990 the team had forty-five days, and in 1994 just one month. Time as tight as this meant zero mistakes and maximum efficiency.

7. **Group dynamics** It isn't necessary to teach national team players how to play football, what is necessary is to make a team. I felt that we had to give the players motivation and equip them with the right psychological approach. I knew someone who ran courses on how to create a team. He was an engineer, not a psychologist – the last thing I wanted was to be accused of using psycho-babble to form the team. The Press would have had a field day if I'd employed a psychologist. Anyway, knowing this man was very good, I invited him to spend some time with us. The results were excellent. He taught us how to improve our technique and mental approach, as well as the importance of being together. He told us that we win matches with twenty-two men, not eleven, and that we were in an enviable position, as thousands of people would love to be representing Brazil at the World Cup. He said we had to be humble, and he used creative examples of team work to demonstrate the importance of working together. For example, a pit stop in Formula One racing takes about eight seconds – that is a team really working together. He said that the difference between success and failure is that when you fail you only give what is requested of you, when you succeed you give 110 per cent. I have to say that this worked miracles; we didn't have any disciplinary problems whatsoever in America, even with players like Romario, who has had disciplinary prob-

lems with his club. Everyone was working together.

8. **Media relationships** I knew we had to live with the media. There were about three hundred journalists travelling with us to America. I dealt with this by being mentally very strong. My attitude, and that of the players was: 'We do what we do, and they will write what they want to write.' We just had to leave them to get on with it and not react to negative or scurrilous reports about our professional or private lives. It's always the same, the journalists want to tell you how to play, who should be selected for the squad, who should play in the team, the positions and strategy we should adopt. I just kept cool and never wavered from my ideals and beliefs.

The players made a suggestion which I thought was very good: they decided that we shouldn't have any Brazilian newspapers in the training camp during the World Cup.

9. **Organization** I ensured that we always had a high standard. In the January before the World Cup we visited America and pre-booked all the hotels and flights; we covered all possibilities. We hired a private plane so that we could travel when it suited us. In some cases we flew out of the city immediately after the game, while the journalists and others had to follow on the next day, by which time we had already had a good night's sleep. Basically, we ensured that the training facilities, the level of physical fitness, the hotel, the technical back-up, the food and the players' sleeping patterns were all maintained to the highest standard. As a nation, we Brazilians haven't always been noted for our ability to organize things efficiently, but this time we really did things well.

10. **Philosophy** I knew that I had to understand the way other countries viewed their football, so I travelled to Germany and England to learn and compare the differences between Brazilian and European football. I knew that the technique of Brazilian players is excellent. After all, twenty play in Europe, and another twenty have the ability to play abroad. Therefore, I allow the player who has the ball to have total freedom to demonstrate his skill; it is the others who don't have the ball who must know exactly what they are doing. The player who has the ball is controlling the game and he has to maintain his speed and go forward until he finds the moment at which he can penetrate the opposition's defence.

My general philosophy was to arrange the team's training to produce the optimum fitness and preparation. We implemented a combination of short and long runs over 100 metres, 200 metres and 300 metres. The players were then divided into groups to run up to 2,000 metres, rest and then repeat down to 500 metres. In total, we had twenty-two sessions of tactical training with seven sections of working on set pieces, i.e. corner kicks and free-kicks. We then had three physical technical sessions and two free days, one in Brazil and two half days in America.

The day before a game we just did recreational training which consists of stretching followed by twenty minutes of touch football.

In the end I think this strategy worked as not only did we win the World Cup, but the media were highly impressed with the fact that not one player mentioned bonuses, they only cared about being World Champions.

I have to say that I disagree with several points. Points 3 and 4 are alright if you are Brazil and you feel you have got the best players and team and are setting the standard for the others. Javier Clemente of Spain decided that to make a very good team even better, he had to increase the odds of winning by changing the tactics. This makes the preparation of the team a lot more difficult, but at least you are armed by playing different systems in the run-up to a major tournament. If there are injuries you can adjust your style of play.

Point 5 shows up the cultural differences. For example, the Brazilian team spontaneously chose to walk out on to the pitch holding hands as a sign of unity. This just wouldn't happen in a northern culture.

Point 6 where Carlos Parreira says that a longer preparation time would be advantageous wouldn't work for us. If our players had to stay together for three months, they would lose concentration, get bored and then lose their edge.

But where you agree or disagree with Parreira, these 10 points were very important to him – and they worked!

Today it is too easy to close down the opposition and play a defensive system, but he chose not to do this. So, tactics haven't entirely caught up talent, rather you need an efficient combination of both talent and organization. The differences between World Cup winners and teams that don't even qualify are getting less. So-called new teams like Japan are already at an acceptable level – as I was going to find out in the summer. Carlos Parreira managed to combine the beauty and freedom of the Brazilian game with organization on the pitch and peace of mind off it. And he came away with the World Cup trophy.

## South Africa

Yvette and I managed to escape to South Africa for a few days' holiday. I don't really take long holidays, but I think it is important to have a small break on a regular basis in order to refresh your mind and put things back in perspective. Joe Mercer used to do this. He always said that he could guarantee that he would come back with something new for the team to work on because he'd had time to think things through.

We stayed in Cape Town in a hotel right under Table Mountain called Mount Nelson. South Africa is naturally a very beautiful place. The fact that the land is rich in precious stones and minerals means that the colour of the earth is very special, and this rich colour pervades every facet of the country. Hopefully, now that apartheid has ended, South Africa will work out its political problems and become a strong international force. Then it really would be paradise on earth. We had a very relaxing time, but I couldn't resist tinkering with my thoughts of our football future. No matter where I go, I think of ways to improve and develop our game.

## Birthday reflections

On 6 January, 1995 I found myself celebrating my fifty-second birthday in Malaysia. I went out to do a couple of seminars and I was invited to their first ever Gala Footballer of the Year dinner. Football is a real passion in the Far East. To show just how important football is to them the Sultan attended the dinner, and I sat next to him and Ossie Ardiles. I'd never really had a chance to talk to Ossie before. The South Americans are very good footballers, technically brilliant, and one very interesting point he made was the difference our cultures have in selecting young footballers.

Our England youth team has always done well because we've chosen big lads, but a lot of those players haven't had the technical ability to match their physical strength and subsequently haven't made it through to senior level. Ossie said that in Argentina and other South American countries, big players don't get chosen if they don't also have the technical ability and a high standard of raw skill. This results in more small players (Ossie says 'football is for small guys'), and kids developing their skill from an early age. This is more logical as when they get to about nineteen or twenty and get physically stronger, the strength and the skill together make an excellent player. But in England the smaller lad is thrown out of preliminary selections for being too small. The guys who select at school level tended in the past to look at the parents, and if they were small then the player would be rejected, as the coaches would presume he wouldn't grow. So, our game tends to be fast, furious and exciting but often lacking in essential skill, especially from the back and into midfield.

I think this is now changing in England. It is vital to encourage skill rather than just physical strength. We have to adapt our game to develop it to meet the needs of playing at international level. We have to get away from our island mentality of thinking that because something has worked in the past then it will still work, and everyone can fit in with us. The last twenty or so years have proved that we are being left behind, and if we want to be a force then we must change and that means changing our ideas at the most basic level, starting off with young kids of seven.

We have weekly doses of Italian football on television, as well as British teams in European competitions, so we can compare our game with theirs, to recognize and develop skills at the earliest age possible. I'm not talking about competitive football – I think that young kids should learn to enjoy playing with a ball before they are told to win at all costs – but rather about getting used to using skill and judgement in playing football and not just kicking the ball as hard as possible. Everything surrounding the game is devoted to winning so there's no need to preach from within. Players like Gazza have developed their skill more by chance than design, and I think we need to have a more organized approach to encouraging children in schools and other organizations.

This exchange of cultural views, chatting to Ossie, is vital in my job. It gives me the chance to get a good overview of how the game is developed in other countries. I hope we become a nation that leads the football world once again. To do this we have to understand what makes the other leading nations great.

## FIFA's Gala Night of the Year

I flew to Lisbon in January to attend FIFA's Gala Night of the Year. This was when the World Footballer of the Year was crowned, and it provided a good opportunity for coaches and other people involved in the game to get together and discuss various pertinent issues.

We had a morning seminar discussion about the finances of top international clubs. This wasn't really my area but I found it illuminating. The presidents of Benfica, Barcelona and Flamengo took the floor and explained that talented players and good football are not necessarily the best road to financial success. It seems that the new sources of revenue, like advertising, sponsorship and marketing are the ways to ensure financial security. That's, of course, why so many clubs produce a new strip each season, or in the case of some clubs who should know better, several new strips. It has the knock-on effect of selling loads of replica strips to thousands of kids who want to be dressed in the latest gear. I'm not sure if I approve of this over-marketing, as it puts unnecessary pressure on mums and dads who haven't always got the money to keep forking out for new kit. At least ticket prices in this country are not high, in comparison to Europe. Ordinary Serie A seats can go for £125 in Italy; even half decent seats are £80 or more. Here, prices respond to supply and demand – if prices are too low, though, it encourages ticket touts.

I am a football man and I understand the merits of producing first-class football on the pitch. I think that kids should be enjoying playing the game and not bothered by who's wearing the latest strip. I'm not against advertising and marketing, but as I have said before, football is not like any other commercial enterprise. That's one of the reasons why Alan Sugar and I fell out. Football is about winning on the pitch and bringing glory to the club; it's not just a hard-nosed business made up of profit and loss accounts. After all, if you earn £5 million but get relegated, are you successful? You can't trade generations of the fans' loyalty for a heavy profit margin. Many fans support the clubs because their fathers did and their grandfathers before them. You have to understand what they want and respect their input in how the club is run, which is why I was always so keen to meet the chairmen of the various supporters' clubs where I've worked, and have a chat with them to get their views on the club and their requirements in terms of facilities at the stadium.

In the afternoon I joined Artur Jorge and Hansi Muller and we did a forum entitled 'Is Attack the Best Form of Defence?' and then we expanded on that and went on into other areas of the game. By this time there seemed to be a major sense-of-humour failure amongst the Press, and when a Spanish journalist asked me, 'What do you think about concepts like ball circulation?' I thought he was in the wrong forum. But we did establish that he was talking about passing the ball, so I was able to explain how the pace of the game in England doesn't always allow the time to demonstrate and develop technique.

In the evening there was the gala dinner, which was in a large marquee. After that we were transferred to a theatre where there was music and entertainment before the announcement of the awards. It all built up towards the World Player of the Year. The president of Portugal was there along with the President of FIFA, João Havelange, and the General Secretary, Sepp Blatter. It shows how important the politicians think sport is, and what a vote winner it can be, when the head of a country comes along to honour not only the great players in his country but also the great international players. In Britain both Conservatives and Labour have issued brochures outlining their philosophies on football, and how they will be contributing to the success of the European Championship finals.

Back in Portugal, Roberto Baggio was voted third in the World Player of the Year, Bulgarian Hristo Stoichkov second, and, not surprisingly, the Brazilian Romario won. The Belgian, Michel Preud'homme won the Goalkeeper of the Year award and the Swedish centre-forward Kennet Andersson was also given an award.

Players like Baggio, Stoichknov and Romario will go down in history as some of the greatest players of this generation of footballers, just as Pelé and Di Stefano did in the past.

I flew back to London with the intention of putting my feet up and watching a video of one of the games as an aid in my preparation for the Ireland match, but instead I flew straight back into the storm of the Kate Hoey Parliamentary declarations.

I must say that I do find it incredible that politicians can be so gullible. If someone put her up to it then I think she got caught up in something much bigger than she realized. Perhaps she wanted to demonstrate that she knew something about football. I don't know what the Shadow Minister for Sport, Tom Pendry, thought of that. He's very good at his job and has a steady hand and is not given to that kind of outburst with little substantiation. Ms Hoey used Parliamentary privilege and I thought that she abused it because I think that she accepted information that came from a newspaper source. Parliamentary privilege is not intended for that purpose and I, and my advisers, are looking into that now. Parliamentary privilege means that within the four walls of Parliament MPs can say what they like and not fear prosecution. They cannot, however, repeat the allegations outside Parliament and enjoy the same privilege. But its purpose was primarily to protect the small individual against the big landowners. It was done to protect the weak against the strong, not to be used as Kate Hoey used it on 30 January 1995. Although attended by only a handful of listeners, her speech was still widely reported in the media.

It is my view that her comments were highly misleading and I could not see any evidence that they had been researched or checked for their validity. She even said, 'Particular credit must be paid to the consistent investigative reporting of Harry Harris of the *Daily Mirror* . . .' Harris has been a constant thorn in our side.

Her statement bore little relation to the facts. Speaking of the 'Clough bung' allegation she asked 'Does the Minister know whether any evidence of financial fraud has been passed on to the police authorities in this case – or indeed any other?'

The reality was that following a complaint by Alan Sugar, the Companies Fraud Squad had exhaustively investigated the matter over a period of some ten months and discontinued their enquiries months before Ms Hoey's speech.

She then accused me of worse offences, stating, 'Indeed, it is possible that he could have contravened the Prevention of Corruption Act 1906. There is certainly clear evidence of the breach of Football Association regulations, in that Venables knew that Eric Hall was acting for him, while at the same time acting for the players.'

I am advised that there are several legal flaws in her assertions, but I will simply say that I inherited Irving Scholar's club policy (presumably sanctioned by the club's board) of using agents, including Eric Hall. My involvement did not breach regulations. Any payment on behalf of the player was a benefit in kind to that player, and the Finance Department at Tottenham should have treated it as such on that player's tax returns.

She also mentioned 'an invoice regarding the transfer of Paul Gascoigne to Lazio for £200,000 . . .', implying that in some way this was dubious. Gino Santin sued *Panorama* over this precise allegation and won substantial damages. The matter had been resolved a whole year before her speech.

# CHAPTER EIGHT

## MATTERS OF SOCIETY, LAW AND POLITICS

The world of football is now highly commercialized and the England team has a major sponsor as well as several official suppliers. The sponsor is a company called Green Flag, which deals with motor vehicle breakdowns. It works on the same principles as the AA and the RAC. Green Flag asked me as England Coach to get involved in doing a television advertisement. I went up to Manchester and they filmed me, Flowers, Ruddock, Shearer, Jones and Pallister at Old Trafford. The FA relies on sponsorship for necessary income and in return companies like Green Flag find that an association with the FA greatly enhances their profile, so it is a highly symbiotic relationship.

We then filmed the second part in Wandsworth, south London, and got there to find there had been a big accident right on the spot where we wanted to film. It was a dreadful accident, one of the worst I've seen, but the driver walked away having completely written his car off. The National Breakdown vehicles had a real-life situation to attend to before they could pose for the ad. But we eventually got all the filming done and then it was off to Wembley where we finished at eight o'clock.

### Paul Merson

Paul Merson made his comeback at the end of January 1995, after a period out of the game due to his problems with addiction to alcohol, drugs and gambling. It was great to see him back. Everyone is always very quick to criticize, especially the Press, but I think people should get a chance in life. I think it was dealt with by the FA in the right way, and I'm sure it was traumatic for him and something he wouldn't want to go through again. People in that situation need help not criticism, and that applies to life as well as sport. I am involved with Turning Point, which helps people with drug problems.

There is a great tendency for the Press to build people up and then take great delight in pulling them down. Fallen heroes sell newspapers, and it sometimes seems as though the Press prefer players to be down on their luck rather than demonstrating their superb skills and ability. I think we could do with a little more help and encouragement and a little less haste in consigning people to the scrap heap. I'm not making excuses for bad behaviour, just saying that when someone is in trouble they need help to overcome their problems, not condemnation.

Turning Point, if you haven't already heard of it, is the largest national charity helping people with drink, drug and mental health problems. It has fifty centres throughout England and Scotland and provides residential care, rehabilitation, day-care and street-level advice and support for those seeking help.

Princess Diana is the patron of Turning Point, but it was set up thirty years ago by Barry Richards. The charity (then known as The Helping Hand Organization) opened the Camberwell Alcohol Project in response to the increasing problem of alcohol misuse. Up until then anyone with an alcohol problem was helped by their local hospital detoxification unit and possibly their local doctor.

I feel very strongly that young people today need help and support to overcome the pressures and problems caused by the fast-living, stressful society we live in. In my day, if you had a problem you'd go and talk to your parents, or to a family friend, and it would get sorted out one way or another. But now most parents are struggling to work and make ends meet, or trying to bring their children up on their own. They don't have time to spend with the kids, who are getting more and more isolated.

Although many parents do a very good job, there are still those who need to take their responsibilities more seriously. The Government should encourage a return to the old team sports, which taught kids, particularly those living in working-class areas, how to work and play. I used to think that the Government had a very weird way of allocating money raised from the National Lottery. Instead of ploughing it into leisure activities that are aimed at improving facilities in working-class areas throughout Britain, it seemed to fund facilities for the privileged few, like the ballet, the opera and the playing fields of Eton.

I went along and had a chat to the top officials at the Department of Heritage, which has sport under its umbrella, and they produced the official figures for the allocation of Lottery money to football. I must say that it is quite impressive. Over nine million pounds has been awarded to various projects: from the development of a new football pitch, disabled access and score-boxes at Wendron Cricket Club, to an all-weather multi-games area with floodlighting, fencing, goals, closed circuit TV, and changing accommodation for Liverpool City Council. In all, 129 organizations have benefited from Lottery money, and I hope this figure increases. It is very important for local communities to have sports facilities. I think we need to have more grass areas in communities on which to play team games. I believe very strongly that Lottery money should *not* be used to build a new National Stadium. The money should be raised from the private business sector, and Lottery money used exclusively to improve facilities throughout the UK.

And surely some of our bigger companies, like Mars or Green Flag, could fund a series of Schools for Excellence in the poorer areas of Britain? The commercial spin-offs from such a project would generate more money and also create a lot of goodwill.

At Turning Point we believe in treating people like individuals, and in the need to get the right balance of rights and responsibilities between the individual and society. There are a lot of people involved in raising money for Turning Point. It is an extremely active charity. Linford Christie, Colin Jackson, Du'aine Ladejo, Chris Boardman, Chris Bonington and the Searle brothers all joined forces to launch Challenge 95, which is an exciting national fitness event to raise money.

Bearing in mind that I believe we should all be doing more to help people who need to lean on us for advice and practical help, I decided to get more involved. Annabel Wilson, the fundraising officer, arranged for me to visit one of their projects in Hackney that provides residential rehabilitation for drug, solvent and alcohol misusers between the ages of seventeen and twenty-five. I learnt a lot of things while I was there, and I was deeply moved and humbled to have contact with these temporarily lost souls. It seemed to me that most of them need a bit of motivating and someone to take an interest in them. These youngsters are our future and we have a responsibility to guide them and help them back on to the straight and narrow. Talking is so important, and if you feel that someone cares, then it makes all the difference to your life. Most of the young people I met were intelligent and wanted to get away from the addictions that had resulted in them seeking help.

The programme they are on usually lasts between six and nine months and combines counselling and group work with a range of practical, educational and leisure-related activities. The sad thing is that many of these young people have been physically, sexually or mentally abused. However, with the help of the facilities at Lorne House, they often make a good recovery before they become too entrenched in substance misuse and the related problems of ill health, homelessness, social breakdown and criminal activity.

One of the most important aspects of the project is to encourage the residents to take equal responsibility for the day-to-day running of the house, including cooking, cleaning and shopping. Incredibly it seems that this is often the first time they have been encouraged to take part in home life. I intend to keep in close touch with developments at Turning Point and hope to become more closely involved in the future.

There are plenty of great alternatives to drugs. Life is for living, and if I can overcome the problems of the last year or two and still keep smiling, then so can the thousands of kids who are hooked on drugs. It's a question of self-esteem, of having pride in yourself. We adults have a responsibility to identify areas where they can expend their energy, and playing football is a great way of keeping fit and using your energy in an intelligent way. You need brain power to play really well; it's a good way of using your brain in connection with your physical skills. I'd like to invite some of the footballing stars to participate in Turning Point projects. I think footballers would help the people who go to Turning Point to understand the good and bad points of social responsibility in life.

Life is never easy, but then if things are too easy they never mean as much. On that note I'll sign off. Little did I realize what was waiting around the corner.

## Blackmail

On Sunday, 5 February, the *Sunday Times* ran headlines screaming VENABLES VICTIM OF £100,000 BLACKMAIL PLOT. This was another chapter in the Venables saga that wouldn't go amiss in a Hollywood film.

There is a thread that runs through my life which is stranger than fiction. This is the dark side of being in the public eye, the side that means you are vulnerable to all kinds of cranks, thieves and downright evil blackmailers, who try and make a quick buck by threatening violence if they don't get what they want.

The Princess of Wales has said she feels there is a plot against her. Maybe I am one of the few people in Britain who can truly understand what she is going through. People accuse her of being paranoid, but as someone once said, 'Just because you're paranoid doesn't mean that people aren't trying to get you!'

This unpleasant business of the blackmail threat started when I was at the England training camp at the end of last year. A man rang me saying that he had some interesting information for me. At first I ignored it as I thought he was just some nutter, then he persisted and started leaving cryptic messages and so I took the call. He had a heavy Irish accent and said he had information about my business dealings and wanted to meet me to discuss it. He told me a few things that made me think he really did know something, and so we agreed to meet.

The meeting place was to be Dirty Dicks, a well-known City pub at Liverpool Street Station. But, as you can imagine, I am not exactly unknown in that area and so it all turned into a bit of a farce. At one stage I wondered if I should disguise myself with a hat and dark glasses, but in the end I just took along my henchman in the shape of my trusted adviser, Eddie Ashby. Of course, as soon as we entered the place an old mate of mine who is also a journalist recognised me and came over to have a chat. I was trying to distance myself but everywhere I turned there seemed to be people I knew, who all wanted to buy me a pint and reminisce about old times. Then this guy approached me and identified himself as the man on the phone. He then quoted facts and figures which demonstrated that he did have access to some confidential documents that had been passed to the Department of Trade and Industry, who were investigating my business affairs after a complaint about me from Alan Sugar.

The man in the pub was able to tell me about all the loans and payments in and out of Edennote (my company), including how I had funded the company, where the money had come from and even when and how I had paid it into the company. What the hell was going on? How did an Irishman have access to supposedly highly confidential Government documents? Of course, it wasn't long before this mystery blackmailer started to make demands for money. He wanted £100,000 to keep his mouth shut. Eddie and I managed to stall him with promises of further meetings, and then we beat a hasty retreat. I contacted my solicitor, Ian Burton, who warned me that the IRA could be behind it. If this was true there was obviously a danger to my life, but I took the decision to go to the police and pursue the matter to the end. I had reached the point where I had to know who was behind this. It seemed as if there were people behind the scenes pulling the strings, and I was determined to flush them out and ensure they received the correct punishment.

The police took it very seriously. They mounted an undercover operation to catch the criminals. I would receive phone calls using coded messages, saying things like 'Meet Mick at the NCP car park on so and so street' and off we went. The police were excellent and kept me fully informed at every stage of the operation.

The police wanted us to arrange a meeting with the Irishman in London, but he obviously got a big windy and refused. So the undercover cops had to go to Ireland disguised as my advisers. The Irish Gardai were then brought in and it was arranged to meet him at one of Dublin's top hotels, The Burlington.

Our chief police contact took the money, £100,000 in cash, over to Dublin. This in itself caused problems as the security machines at Heathrow Airport picked up the fact that someone was taking a briefcase full of money to Dublin and they tried to make him open the case. The undercover cop wanted to stay undercover, but he was forced to show his ID before being allowed to proceed to the aircraft.

The meeting took place as arranged at The Burlington, between two Scotland Yard Officers posing as my business associates, and the man who had the computer disk on which he claimed was a list of all my business dealings. The Irish Gardai were hiding in side rooms with automatic guns and black hoods hiding their faces.

There was a slight hiccup when the two Scotland Yard men couldn't get the laptop computer to work. They struggled for ages, while the Gardai were sweating it out in the side rooms wondering what on earth was going on. Eventually, they got it to work and sure enough there was the tape which had been passed to the DTI. The London cops negotiated hard with the blackmailer, and he agreed to accept £80,000 in cash. They opened the briefcase, and the Irishman's mouth fell open.

His last words were 'Christmas has come early.' Then the Irish Gardai charged out of the rooms and caught him bang to rights with the tape and about to take the money.

Unfortunately, the whole distressing episode has still not been resolved. I understand that as well as the question of theft, it is a criminal offence to disclose contents or a confidential report under 447 of the Companies Act. The Irishman has not been charged, neither has the woman who worked in the DTI office, and sent it to the man, who was her brother, in the hope of making a quick buck. Why the hell haven't they been charged?

Although the police took the computer disk, I cannot believe that this villain hasn't made a copy. That means that he has valuable information to sell to anyone who is interested in my affairs and can use this confidential information against me. It makes me wonder if someone has paid for the disk and that is the reason why there have been so many leaks in newspapers like the *Daily Telegraph* and the *Daily Mirror*. The *Independent* of 1 February 1996 ran an article on how documents from the DTI and Serious Fraud Office were also seen by journalists.

The fact is that a woman Government official can send a confidential computer disk through the DTI official postal system to her brother in Ireland with the sole objective of making money, get caught in the act and yet escape conviction.

# CHAPTER NINE

## DUBLIN DÉBÂCLE

**Republic of Ireland v England**
**The Squad**
David Seaman – Arsenal
Ian Walker – Tottenham Hotspur
Warren Barton – Wimbledon
Tony Adams – Arsenal
Steve Howey – Newcastle United
Sol Campbell – Tottenham Hotspur
Gary Pallister – Manchester United
Stuart Pearce – Nottingham Forest
Graeme Le Saux – Blackburn Rovers
Darren Anderton – Tottenham Hotspur
Robert Lee – Newcastle United
Tim Sherwood – Blackburn Rovers
Paul Ince – Manchester United
David Platt – Sampdoria
Nick Barmby – Tottenham Hotspur
Peter Beardsley – Newcastle United
Matthew Le Tissier – Southampton
Ian Wright – Arsenal
Les Ferdinand – Queen's Park Rangers
Teddy Sheringham – Tottenham Hotspur
Alan Shearer – Blackburn Rovers

I was so encouraged by the general progress that we were making that I decided to push through some more complicated tactical changes. We didn't have much time and I decided to do more work on the blackboard rather than on the pitch.

I was trying to draw Ince backwards into the back two players and get the full-backs forward. I wanted the full-backs wide, ready to go forward, but this did not work on the night!

REPUBLIC OF IRELAND V ENGLAND 15 February 1995
Lansdowne Road, Dublin
Attendance: 46,000
Republic of Ireland: A Kelly, Irwin, Phelan, Kernaghan, McGrath, Staunton, Sheridan, D Kelly, Quinn, Townsend, McGoldrick
England: Seaman, Barton, Le Saux, Platt, Pallister, Beardsley, Ince, Shearer, Le Tissier, Anderton
Scorer: D Kelly
Game abandoned after 27 minutes.

England v Ireland was my first away match and it was going to be a chance for me to try out a few new theories and see what we were like away from home (not that I wanted an away game at that time). Unfortunately other events overtook the footballing side and once again left the English with a tarnished image abroad.

As you can imagine, I was bitterly disappointed by the outcome, as not only were we denied the chance to show our full capabilities, but once again, the behaviour of people who are clearly not football fans ruined the game for everyone.

Pictures of rioting English fans were flashed around the world. I felt sickened by the scenes. I thought we had left all that behind and had moved on towards behaving in a civilized fashion. It was made even worse by the fact that it happened in Ireland, where the Irish fans are known for their enthusiastic but tolerant behaviour. As I watched the scenes on television later that night, I remembered the different images that had come from the 1990 World Cup, when Ireland had played the host country, Italy, in the magnificent Olympic Stadium. Italy won the match, but both sets of fans celebrated by dancing in the streets and frolicking in the fountains of central Rome, their arms locked round each other. It had been a great sporting occasion and the behaviour of both sets of fans had reflected this. What a pity we are blighted by a few mindless cretins.

I thought we were probably caught off-guard, having been lulled into a false sense of security. I never dreamt that anything like that could happen again, although when I went out on the pitch during the team warm up, I noticed a very aggressive group of guys to my right, and alarm bells went off in my head. This wasn't just a few football fans getting revved up for the game, it seemed different, much more sinister.

Then I put it out of my mind – I had to get my thoughts together for the game – and as we walked back down the tunnel I was concentrating on the match rather than what was going on in the stands. However, when the violence flared, my mind immediately flashed back to those guys. There were three or four of them giving abuse to anyone they could get within mouthing distance of. They were big guys with woollen hats pulled down over their eyes and really acting in a very aggressive manner. But I thought security would have it under control.

Anyway, back to the game. I am the first to admit that I made mistakes in this match. My original instinct that too many discussions round the blackboard rather than on the pitch leads to confusion was proved right. We were all over the place. Although the game lasted only twenty-seven minutes, I could see where I had to correct the mistakes and, in fact, the first thing I did when were were called back to the dressing-room was to put things right.

I wanted to do a few things that were too complex. If I'd had a few more games, then I wouldn't have had to do it all in this match. I've always kept things simple in the past and that taught me a lesson. Usually, I would have worked with the players for five or six days before implementing the changes I made in the Ireland match, but instead I crammed it in over two days.

We just weren't comfortable. We were getting our full-backs not only too wide but also too far forward, then when we lost the ball our centre-halves were the only ones there to retrieve the situation. It put too much pressure on them: they had to get wider than normal as the ball came forward, rather than waiting for it. Tactically, it was easy to put right, and the players agreed with me as soon as I had a chat to them back in the dressing-room.

I don't regret this mistake as I think you have to be bold and try and implement new things. If you never try anything you'll never know if it works or not. The mistake here was not to try it out on the pitch first. You can't play safe every game. At least we can learn from our mistakes. Up until now there had been far more pluses than minuses.

Regarding the trouble, I remember someone shouting, 'They're throwing things on the pitch,' and then the referee brought the players off. He acted completely correctly; there was no alternative. Jack and I met in the corridor outside the changing-rooms. He said to me, 'Do you want to play on?' I said, 'Yes,' and we thought that once the pitch had been cleared we'd be able to resume the match. We didn't realize just how serious it had become.

Meanwhile, the referee was standing by us, listening to our comments about playing on and looking very unhappy. He was shaking his head and, although he hadn't made any decision, it was obvious that there wasn't much chance of carrying on. Then the police called the match off on grounds of safety.

To say that I was disappointed was an understatement! The game that I'd been planning and looking forward to for months had just gone up in smoke. It wasn't just that game that I lost, but a chance to build the team. I only had two games, the next one being against Uruguay, before the summer tournament with Brazil, Japan and Sweden, which was vital preparation for the European Championship.

I just have to go with my experience and trust my gut reaction to decide if the various changes I want to make are right or not. The main thing is not to be pressurized by the Press. Being a bunch of frustrated England coaches they always think things can be done better; the problem is they usually only have half, or less, of the information that I have about the players who are available to me. Of course, I'm not infallible, but I would have liked the chance to see what would have happened once the players had gone out and reorganized themselves at Lansdowne Road.

However, I'm not criticizing the police decision; they knew what was going on and how serious it was, and they had to do what they felt was right. I was just fed up from a footballing angle, although I knew it was a secondary consideration. If it had been a competitive game, then the stadium would have been cleared and we would have played on, but the police were worried that the fans would be difficult to control if the game was still being played. So we went home in disgrace and with absolutely nothing proved on the pitch.

Politically, it is clear that these people are not football fans; no one who cares about their club would behave in that way. I also

think it is a misguided attitude from the people in authority who
think this is solely a football problem. Who can say that these same
political groups, for that is what they are, won't attach themselves
to other sports, like rugby or cricket? It's certainly not a drink
problem as the rugby fans drink all day and still have a jovial attitude. No, these troublemakers are organized and determined to
cause maximum problems. They know that football is our highest
profile sport, and causing a riot is the best way to get the most
publicity.

The police and others knew what was happening and also, that
there is tension between these right-wing political groups and the
IRA. I think they should have been a bit more prepared for trouble.
We seem to be too wimpish in dealing with this kind of problem,
and direction, strong direction for a forceful deterrent has to come
from the highest Government sources, even the Prime Minister.
We mustn't make excuses for this kind of behaviour. If it is repeated
during the European Championship finals, then, in social terms, we
will be the disgrace of the world. It won't matter if we win the
European Championship; it will all mean nothing if it is overshad-
owed by pictures of thugs throwing bits of iron down from the terraces and fighting in the streets. That will undermine my efforts and
the efforts of everyone connected with the England team.

It's not football's failure and rugby's success. A lot of journalists agree with me that it is a political problem, and then some
write the exact opposite, and I read that it's football's problem. It
isn't. We all have to take responsibility for stamping it out, including the people who know who is causing trouble and keep quiet.
That is almost as criminal as the act of violence. In this world you
have to stand up and be counted. It's a philosophy I have always
followed, even if it has sometimes cost me dear, in financial and
personal terms, but you have to fight for what is right, even if the
odds are stacked against you.

I wanted to come away from Ireland with some positive
thoughts and ideas that I could use in future games, but there
were no thoughts of football in my head as we drove away from
Lansdowne Road, just an overwhelming feeling of sadness and disgust. I felt empty as I reflected on how something so big could be
brought down by so few. There was a full house, that meant over
40,000 people in the stadium, and it was all ruined by two or three
hundred delinquents.

The new England Coach meets the Press at Wembley Stadium on 28 January 1994 (© *Popperfoto*)

Terry watches the England squad go through their paces in training
(© *Popperfoto*)

Terry with England captain David Platt at Bisham Abbey before England v Denmark, Terry's first game as England Coach (© *Popperfoto*)

Terry jokes with Paul Gascoigne on his arrival from Italy to join the England squad at Bisham Abbey, March 1994 (© *Popperfoto*)

Terry and Don Howe at Bisham Abbey (© *Popperfoto*)

Helping Lennox Lewis with his belts at Bisham Abbey in March 1994 are
Anderton, Le Saux, Le Tissier and Terry (© *Popperfoto*)

Terry and his dad Fred, at the launch of The Manager board game
(© *Ray Pickard Photography*)

Terry and schoolchildren at the launch of the Mars Snickers 1994 campaign to
promote football at grass roots level (© *Pic Photos Ltd*)

Terry presenting Eric Cantona with the Player of the Year Award at the PFA
Awards in April 1994 (© *Popperfoto*)

Terry, Ted Buxton and Jimmy Hill at the PFA Awards in April 1994 discuss
'Old McDonald's Farm' (© *Popperfoto*)

Terry discusses the media with David Davies, Director of Public Affairs for the
FA (© *Eddie Keogh*)

Terry with Denmark's Richard Møller-Nielson and the trophy at the Euro 96
launch in October 1994 (© *Popperfoto*)

Terry and Bryan Robson watching England training in Dublin, February 1995
(© *Popperfoto*)

Terry and David Davies devastated after rioting England fans ended the
Republic of Ireland v England match after 27 minutes, 15 February 1995
(© *Popperfoto*)

I think we will have to consider banning travelling supporters, which is unfair to the true supporters, but it might be the lesser of the two evils. If we don't get a grip, we'll end up not having any games at all, either home or away. I don't think they should cancel the European Championships, because who's to say that a similar thing wouldn't happen in Italy or Germany. You have to refuse to be beaten. Tournaments can't be cancelled because we're too frightened of the consequences. When you don't have any problems, you don't have a life!

As I've mentioned, it has always been my view that we have to provide facilities in poor areas so that kids can play ball games and learn to enjoy themselves in a healthier environment. It's no good having kids cooped up in high-rise apartment blocks and not providing them with some way to use up their energy and abilities to organize themselves.

Both the Conservative and Labour documents on football cover the thorny problem of hooliganism. Tom Pendry, the Shadow Minister for Sport and Tourism, sets out the Labour position regarding violence:

> We believe that there needs to be legislation produced to tighten up the present legislative orders. We have to act to combat this type of mindless violence. Over the last three years only three restrictive orders have been issued. At the time of the Dublin riot only two were actually in force and one of these was not acted upon. We want to toughen up the measures to enforce and increase the level of punishment applicable for failing to meet the terms of an order by substantially increasing the penalty to an equivalent £2,500 fine or 45 days imprisonment.
>
> One of our main concerns is to deal effectively with acts of violence committed abroad. Too often foreign governments are so browned off with hooligan behaviour that they just round up the offenders and put them on the first plane back home. Unfortunately, this doesn't help us. We believe that those guilty of hooliganism should be prosecuted in the country where the crime is committed. If other countries fail in their obligation, then hooligans should be brought to trial in England and Wales under Section 22 of the Football Spectators Act (1989) and Article 5 of the European Convention

on Spectator Violence, which we have signed up to support.

We think we, i.e. Labour, should take a lead in ensuring that member states who have signed up to the convention should adhere to it. That means troublemakers will be either tried abroad and then placed on a register in this country, or shipped back to England once charged to face trial here. The main consequence of this is that if found guilty, the offender would have to report to a police station at a certain time on the day of a designated match. This would keep him away from the match and rid the game of these undesirables.

As well as being tougher on legislation, we also want to fight against racist chanting, obscenity chanting and the inciting of violence. At the moment, to be charged requires one person against another (there is no mention of crowd violence) and we think that should be tightened up.

I was shocked by the scenes that came out of the Ireland v England match in Dublin. Although it is up to football to put its own house in order, the role of Government is to establish a framework in which football can thrive, and the present Government is just not doing enough in this area. We have to act to stamp out this violence and ensure that people who visit England during the 1996 European Championship finals will come away with a positive image of the game and our country.

Of course the government feels it is handling things effectively, and having talked to the Department of Heritage I have to say that I am impressed with their plans on the security front as far as England is concerned. The Taylor Report resulted in a massive investment in the improvement of the stadiums. The Government ploughed £136 million into football following the report. This was money raised from the deduction in betting duty from the pools companies.

Security concerning the European Championship finals is already in place. Our police force has a great deal of experience and there is a vast inter-police network of information being passed around. If a fan arrives with a known criminal record then he or she can be prevented from entering the country on the grounds of being a threat to public order.

There will be spotters who will watch known troublemakers the whole time. This allays my fears somewhat. We have already suffered several periods of disgrace: now it is time for action to ensure that dreadful scenes like those in Dublin never happen again.

## The Dennis Wise Case

Before we could catch breath after the Irish riots, Dennis Wise went to court and was sentenced to three months imprisonment for assault. This would mean that he would be out of the summer tournament. I knew he would be devastated by this.

I feel I should make a few comments about this as I saw Dennis on the night of the incident – in my club, Scribes. I think there are mitigating circumstances and that, in this case, Dennis was treated too harshly and held up as an example.

There is one thing for certain: Dennis was not drunk. I saw him at about eleven-thirty as he came to pick up his football boots from his agent Eric Hall, who had had them delivered to him from Puma. I spoke to him for about fifteen minutes and he was fine, in good form, laughing and joking and being his usual bubbly self. He certainly wasn't being aggressive or argumentative about anything. I know because I talked to him, but from the news coverage I thought that I was reading about a different incident.

After the incident it was alleged that it had been settled out of court for something like a thousand or two thousand pounds. The cab driver didn't want to press charges and the police who dealt with it didn't want to proceed further, then it seemed that someone higher up in the police force decided to go on with it. And so he ended up in court. I don't want to make excuses for someone if they misbehave, but it seems strange that the fact his girlfriend was knocked over in the commotion wasn't taken into consideration. Anyone would react if their family or close friends were about to be hurt or injured in some way. If Yvette had been knocked over I would have reacted very angrily. If Dennis was regularly in trouble I would agree that he needed to be taught a short, sharp lesson, but it doesn't seem as if this was the case.

# CHAPTER TEN

## GAZZA'S BACK

My admiration for Paul Gascoigne is no secret. He is one of our most gifted players and although he is a difficult player to handle, I have always found that his positive points far outweigh the hassles of managing him.

However, Gazza's career has been dogged by injury. First there was the knee injury sustained during the FA Cup final when I was manager of Tottenham, then there was the injury to his kneecap, which resulted from an incident in a nightclub in Newcastle. Finally, he broke his leg last year whilst training for Lazio. But there is one great thing about Gazza – he always bounces back. His strength and determination to fight back are second to none. His uninhibited enthusiasm for life has its positive and negative aspects. During the negative phases he can become self-destructive, but the positive side of his character means that he gives everything to getting fit again.

At the beginning of March 1994, I spoke to him quite a few times. He was full of bounce and optimism, he was training hard and said that he would return to playing football by April. To find out more about the likely date of his return to the game, I went to see top orthopaedic surgeon, John Browett, who has the dubious pleasure of being known in the trade as 'Gazza's doctor'. He is the man who has dedicated many a weekend to mending some part of Gazza's broken body and is therefore able to describe his physical state of readiness better than anyone else.

John Browett is not only a brilliant surgeon but a man with a strong sense of humour, which I am sure has been sorely tested over the years! When I saw him in his private treatment rooms in Harley Street, he was feeling very positive about Gazza's ability to make a full return to the game by the end of the 94-95 season. He said to me, 'I would have preferred to keep him away from playing in a competitive match until the beginning of next season, but as he is doing so well, I don't think it would be fair to keep him away any longer than absolutely necessary.'

One of his main problems has been pacing the player so he didn't run before he could walk again. John is very fond of Gazza and has a high opinion of his ability to dedicate himself to getting fit again, but he did admit that having him as a patient was a bit like riding a runaway stallion bareback. You always felt you could slip off at any time and lose control of the beast.

John Browett explained, 'After the fractured patella, I gated him in his house. John Sheridan (Tottenham's physio, who was given special responsibility for Gazza's rehab) and I sat down with him and explained that if the wound didn't heal that would be the end of his career, and if it wasn't given time and rest to do this, then it wouldn't heal. To give him his credit Gazza took us very seriously and remained in his house in Hoddeston for six weeks. I understand that he watched every single video from the local video shop to try and relieve the boredom, but he stuck it out and that saved his career.'

I'm very pleased he took his advice so seriously. England needs him and I am looking forward to when Gazza will make a full contribution to the England team again. There aren't too many players around with Gazza's skill and boundless joy for the game. When he's on form, there isn't anyone who can stop him, and he has a football intelligence and drive that can change games. His mental drive is incredible: if the other players are losing the game and starting to put their heads down, it is Gazza who will rally them round and keep the confidence going. There isn't too high a value you can put on that.

Everything was going well. Gazza returned to play for Lazio, winning the man of the match award on at least two occasions. He seemed to have overcome his injuries and have rehabilitated well. At international level you have to possess a high level of physical ability and have the right physical/mental link-up to have reflexes that can react fast enough. He played well against Denmark in spite of the fact that he was nursing a slight injury. But then disaster struck again.

On Thursday, 7 April, 1994, he fractured his right tibia in a training incident at Lazio's Maestrelli training ground. It was simply a clash of shins with a young Lazio player. The reason that Gazza smashed his leg and the other guy didn't could be put down to age. The other guy was only eighteen, which is an age when the bones are still young and fairly flexible. Although not exactly an old age pensioner, Gazza was coming up to twenty-seven and his bones were beginning to be a bit more set if not quite as creaky as mine!

John Browett confirmed that this new injury certainly wasn't caused by any weakness due to the previous injuries. On Friday, 8 April Gazza flew into London and the next day John Browett once more operated on his leg.

The original prognosis was that he would be out of the game for a year and, as we sat in John's office on Monday, 6 March, 1995, he confirmed that he was right on target.

'He's very fit. I've seen some photos of him training and he looks very impressive. Maurizio Manzini of Lazio keeps me informed about his progress. Lazio are delighted with him. He is now down to seventy-two kilos in weight, that means he's lost sixteen kilos in total, which is incredible. I don't think I can stop him from returning to play football before the end of the season.'

That made me feel good as it meant that Gazza should be available for the pre-European Championship tournament at the beginning of June. It would give me a chance to see how he was shaping up.

On my last trip to Rome, just after I was appointed England Coach in 1994, I found a different Gazza from the one I knew at Tottenham. John Browett has also been suitably impressed by the change over the years. He said that he found Gazza much easier to deal with now, and more willing to accept John's decisions.

As I got up to leave John's office, he said, 'Gazza has done exceptionally well to fight his way back to fitness from such a series of serious injuries. You must be proud of him.'

As I walked down the steps and out into the pouring rain, I reflected on the fact that, yes, I was very proud of Gazza, and in a funny way fighting back to fitness had saved him. If he hadn't had these injuries maybe he would have carried on being the old, reckless Gazza, prone to wildness and unpredictable behaviour. Maybe the challanges that life had thrown up at him had resulted in a much more thoughtful and reflective man. We all have ways of coping with adversity; Gazza had shown us that the best way is just to keep your head down and get on with building up your life. I thought about the problems I'd been through and decided that the best way you can cope is to never give up in believing in yourself. However, just when you think you've beaten the problem, it can come back. Gazza must keep on top of his underlying problems if he is going to keep everyone's faith in him. The self-destruct button is always there. If you don't keep on top of it, someone will push it for you!

# CHAPTER ELEVEN

## ENGLAND V URUGUAY

There always seems to be controversy surrounding every match, and this time the Press were making a big deal out of the fact that I had left out Matthew Le Tissier from the squad.

In all fairness, it has to be said that he hadn't been playing to his best for quite a long time. When that type of player is not doing what he does best, like scoring goals, or showing the magic he has, then there is no guarantee that he will be able to make a difference to any team.

I'd be a fool if I couldn't recognize his talents and he's a good player. It's just a matter of opinion and it's mine that counts at the moment. As I'm leaving at the end of the European Championship, maybe there will be a new chance for Matt. I think that skill by itself is never enough. Many gifted players have failed to maximize their great potential. I believe that determination is the characteristic common to all great players. The American President Calvin Coolidge said: 'Nothing in the world can take the place of consistence, talent will not. Nothing is more common than unsuccessful men with talent. Determination and consistence alone are omnipotent.'

And if you think about it, the really great players have all had strength and determination; Pelé, Best, Cruyff. You can't substitute skill for work rate, but to succeed you need both. People want to take things too literally. If you claim you can't win anything at the top level without discipline, you get headlines in the tabloid newspapers about forming a team of robots. But that is just ignorance. It doesn't mean that if you have discipline the style of play has to suffer, rather that the great teams have all had a framework to build on. For example, the great Brazilian side of 1970 had an organized way of playing through Zagelo, and then they could continue to play a cavalier type of game using skill, but within a set discipline. And, as we've already seen, Carlos Alberto Parreira knew that to win the 1994 World Cup he had to harness discipline and team work. He was determined that the star of the team would be the team; in other words there would be no individual stars just eleven players who all worked well together for the good of the team not for their own individual glory.

Therefore you can't take a chance on a skilful player who isn't performing to his best. What you need are skilful players who can contribute a high degree of efficiency to the team; that means players like Anderton, Gascoigne and Shearer. These players are examples of highly skilled technicians who are at clubs that still stretch them and make them work. In my opinion, I really don't think that his club manager at Southampton, Alan Ball, was doing Le Tissier any favours by keeping on about what a great player he is. I prefer not to over-praise a player, so he is stretched and performs at his best.

To achieve the heights you have to accept some pain. I feel that there are certain players who, when confronted with the pain barrier, back away from it. I want a team of players who can adapt when things get a little tough, fight on and go through it and not just sit on their laurels thinking I'm too good to get stuck in, I can't be bothered to help out the rest of the team.

Paul Gascoigne is a prime example of a player who will get stuck in. When the chips are down he gets his head down and fights back either on or off the pitch. He had a weight problem, and so he set about overcoming it. Mind you, he's now gone to the other extreme and become obsessed with fitness and diets. It's all he talks about! He's begining to sound like a supermodel. I half expect to see him on one of those afternoon chat shows swapping diet secrets with Kate Moss.

Since I had first implemented a system we called the Christmas tree, we had evolved, even though the changes were subtle. However, I still expect the guys who write about the game to be up-to-date with the system I am using! The Christmas tree had a 4-3-2-1 formation, whereas now we were using a 4-1-3-1-1 with Venison in the holding position in front of the back four. During the World Cup, seventeen out of the twenty-four teams used a striker up front with a player just behind him. This has thrown a lot of defence systems out of the window.

### The Squad
Tim Flowers – Blackburn Rovers
Ian Walker – Tottenham Hotspur
Rob Jones – Liverpool
Warren Barton – Wimbledon
Tony Adams – Arsenal
Steve Howey – Newcastle United
Gary Pallister – Manchester United
Neil Ruddock – Liverpool
Graeme Le Saux – Blackburn Rovers
Stuart Pearce – Nottingham Forest
Darren Anderton – Tottenham Hotspur
Robert Lee – Newcastle United
Barry Venison – Newcastle United
David Platt – Sampdoria
Tim Sherwood – Blackburn Rovers
Jamie Redknapp – Liverpool
John Barnes – Liverpool
Steve McManaman – Liverpool
Nick Barmby – Tottenham Hotspur
Peter Beardsley – Newcastle United
Teddy Sheringham – Tottenham Hotspur
Andy Cole – Manchester United

Now that I have a strategy I have to decide who will play in the various positions, and what I am trying to do is to achieve a bit of consistency in the team and form a side that will last two years. I brought in the youngsters, Anderton and Le Saux, and they have been brilliant, but they wouldn't have fitted in so well if they hadn't had the advantage of the experience of such players as Beardsley and Platt. I am also trying to get a smooth switch over from the Under-21s to the senior side.

I have earmarked Robbie Fowler, Jamie Redknapp, Sol Campbell and Nick Barmby for future development, and some of these players like Darren Anderton have already got into the senior side on their own merits. Fowler could have been in but he's suffered suspension. But I have already got Barmby in to start learning from Beardsley, and Redknapp has been introduced to the senior side. Sol Campbell couldn't play against Uruguay as he was injured. But these youngsters are all learning their business at the top end of things by being around the experienced players.

I really do think this takeover period is very important. Beardsley had a great 94/95 season, his passing ability and knowledge of the game is still great. With players like him you just have to wait and see how things develop as time goes by. If they are able to continue, that's good, if not, they can pass on their experience to the younger players coming into the squad.

My main objective as we went into the match against Uruguay was to consolidate things as far as the integration between old players and new was concerned, and continue to tune finely our team in readiness for the summer tournament.

We have already discussed the role of the doctor, but since there is such an emphasis on the way diet relates to fitness and people are curious to know what we eat, here's an example of some of the pre-match training camp fare at Burnham Beeches. The doctor decides on the menus a week before we arrive, after consulting the hotel.

**THURSDAY**

| Supper | Tomato Soup |
| | Filled rolls and sandwiches |

**FRIDAY**

| Breakfast | Fresh fruit juice |
| | Cereal |
| | Toast or danish pastry |
| *or* | Bacon, well-done |
| | Scrambled egg |
| Lunch | Chicken soup |
| | Lasagne *or* omelette |
| | Mixed salad |
| | Ice cream |
| Supper | Soup *or* prawn cocktail |
| | Small portion of spaghetti bolognaise |
| | Fillet steak, well-done *or* grilled salmon |
| | Thick-cut chips |

Peas, beans and broccoli
Apple tart
Custard
Cheese and biscuits

**SATURDAY**
Breakfast             Fresh fruit juice
                      Cereal
                      Toast or danish pastry
*or*                  Bacon, well-done
                      Scrambled egg
Lunch                 Soup
                      Selection from cold meat, prawns, baked
                      potato, salad, cottage pie
                      Fruit salad and ice cream *or* rice pudding

Here we break up and meet again on Sunday night:
**SUNDAY**
Supper                Tomato soup
                      Filled rolls and sandwiches

**MONDAY**
Breakfast             Fresh fruit juice
                      Cereal
                      Toast or danish pastry
*or*                  Bacon, well-done
                      Scrambled egg
Lunch                 Oxtail soup
                      Grilled chicken breasts
                      Mashed potatoes
                      Carrots, peas, sweetcorn
                      Gravy
                      Fruit salad and ice cream
Supper                Cream of celery soup
                      Small portion of lasagne
                      Grilled steak, well-done *or* grilled white fish
                      Thick-cut chips
                      Vegetable of the day
                      Rice pudding *or* mixed fruit crumble

**TUESDAY**
Breakfast             Fresh fruit juice
                      Cereal

|        | Toast or danish pastry |
|--------|------------------------|
| *or*   | Bacon, well-done       |
|        | Scrambled egg          |
| Lunch  | Tomato soup            |
|        | Omelette *or* cottage pie |
|        | Peas, baked beans      |
|        | Fruit salad and ice cream |
| Supper | Minestrone soup and rolls |
|        | Small portion spaghetti bolognaise |
|        | Braised beef           |
|        | Gravy                  |
|        | Mashed potatoes        |
|        | Mixed vegetables       |
|        | Rice pudding *or* fruit salad and ice cream |

*Extras*

Players are allowed to provide their own extras such as chocolate, biscuits, danish pastries to supplement their desserts.

| **MATCH DAYS** | Pasta |
|----------------|-------|
|                | Chicken *or* fish |
|                | Potatoes |

There are certain things that are put on each table before each meal: fresh fruit, brown sauce, tomato sauce, mustard, margarine and soft drinks. I know this is a bit different from Italy or Spain, but even though the English have moved towards a more nutritious and controlled diet, we still follow certain tastes and conventions. We can compare our diet to, say, the Italians and we would see that they concentrate almost exclusively on the benefits of a Mediterranean diet. We have an improved diet but it is still essentially Anglicized. The Italians have a lot more of the two 'superfoods': pasta and fresh fruit. We haven't yet got round to getting the players to eat a fresh pear after training, just as the players don't feel entirely happy about being locked up together for six consecutive days. It's just a case of having a different philosophy, but I do think it would be enormously beneficial for our players and managers to spend some time abroad. We need to expand out minds and learn languages. We can't go on being so insular. But there are plans afoot to start encouraging our kids to take an interest in our European neighbours.

ENGLAND V URUGUAY Wednesday 29 March 1995
Wembley Stadium
Attendance: 34,849
England: Flowers, Jones, Le Saux (McManaman 46), Venison, Adams, Pallister, Platt, Beardsley (Barmby 65), Sheringham (Cole 71), Barnes, Anderton
Uruguay: Ferro, Aguirregaray, Gutierrez, Lopez, Dorta, Montero, Cedras, Bengoechea, Fonseca, Francescoli (Debray 85), Poyet
Result: 0–0
Referee: H Krug (Germany)

There was much criticism of this game from the Press and public, but a much more rational view should be taken. As Neil Harman wrote in the *Daily Mail*: 'We saw a South American team of considerable talent have not one shot at target and we witnessed the extension of Terry Venables' unbeaten record as head coach to seven matches.'

There is little doubt, however, that the game did not live up to expectations. It could be said that expectations were simply too high. After the débâcle of the Irish game, many fans wanted to see England's reputation restored with a high-scoring win, but realistically this was never going to be the case.

There was the much-awaited appearance of Andy Cole, who previously came into the squad for one of our get-togethers, and was then unavailable due to injury. He gave us a glimpse of what he could do. He was unlucky not to have scored from a shot which hit the crossbar.

I felt that when we were making our forward runs we were over-cautious, as though concerned we'd have to get back instead of commiting ourselves and going for it and really worrying the opposition. I don't think our runs were positive enough and I was disappointed in this.

Sheringham and Beardsley had good chances in the first half and we had four good ones in the second half, through Anderton, Beardsley, Sheringham and Cole – two from Anderton. But we still didn't manage to finish off. Uruguay were very well organized with good technical players but they weren't unbeatable.

The crowd was frustrated – they wanted to see us score! They would have preferred to see a 2–2 scoreline, but I think we should ensure we are solid. I now know where we need to improve and that's what we'll concentrate on without forgetting the organization at the back.

One thing I would like to correct is what the Uruguayan coach, Hector Nunez, said about England. What he actually stated was that we were lacking a playmaker, but certain sections of the Press chose to misinterpret it and so we saw headlines about us being 'brainless'.

In fact, we had John Barnes in the position of playmaker, and I have to disagree with Mr Nunez, as I thought that he did quite well. The thing about Barnes is that however much flak he gets, he always sticks to his guns, and I respect that.

Uruguay weren't unbeatable, but we mustn't forget that they have some outstanding players, such as Francescoli and Fonseca. Fonseca was amazing in a game against Spain, he scored a great goal and had an even better one disallowed. I think we did very well in denying him a goal-scoring opportunity.

I really do think we got better as the game went on. Anderton, Pallister and Adams all played well, and Venison did well in the first half. Unfortunately, I hadn't got the full-back position covered by the subs as I knew I'd need greater support in midfield, so it was a big problem when Le Saux came off injured. We had to sort out some big changes for the second half. Venison had to play at right-back and Barnes moved into the centre of midfield. Jones came on at left-back and did very well, and Venison slotted into the right-back position with no problems. Barnes moved into the centre of midfield. It's a pity Venison moved to Turkey when he did as I think he still had something to give England, but that move put him out of the frame of things, as it is difficult to keep in touch on a regular basis, and with an older player you need to keep a close eye on his club form. However, with his return from Southampton, he has put himself back in the swing of things. A player with Venison's talent and experience is always useful.

But considering the opposition, I was not unhappy at the score-line. Though after the match I thought of our get-together at the end of April, and of bringing in some of the other strikers like Stan Collymore and Chris Sutton to have a look at what they can do.

People expect miracles but after this match I was pleased with the way things were going. In my mind I have a scheme and it is all beginning to fit into place.

# Chapter Twelve

## Around Football

The Eric Cantona case was settled and Eric was sentenced to 120 hours of community service after winning an appeal against a fourteen-day jail sentence.

My views on the incident have already been recorded. I think the game desperately needs an extendable tunnel which would come out on to the pitch to keep a distance between the players and the fans. This is commonly used on the Continent and I really don't understand why we can't get our act together over here. I was disgusted by the incident during which a fan spat at my predecessor, Graham Taylor. This is a gross, vulgar act of disrespect, and I wouldn't have blamed Graham if he had lost his temper even more than he did. With a moving tunnel this wouldn't have occurred.

True to form, Eric gave us all something to think about at the press conference after his sentence had been overturned. 'When the seagulls follow the trawler it is because they think sardines will be thrown into the sea.' Well, that gave all the psychologists something to think about. And it gave the rest of us a bit of light relief. I was amused to read some of the psychologists' comments. Raj Persaud said, 'He wants to keep people guessing because he thinks he is better than everyone else. Basically, in sea terms, he is saying he is bigger than your average sardine. The seagulls are undoubtedly the people in the media who were hoping to see him go to prison . . . Behind the remark are his feelings of being superior. He wants to think there are a lot of people trying to work out what he meant. He doesn't like being ignored.'

Whereas Professor Percy Cohen, a psychology and rationality

lecturer at the London School of Economics, said Cantona was demonstrating 'pure defiance'. The professor declared: 'The man is saying, "I will be back and I will be back a stronger man, and in charge of what I am doing." It is really quite eloquent and shows he is not mad at all, despite what everyone might think.'

Well, I am not going to enter into the realms of whether Eric Cantona is mad or not, but he is different both on and off the pitch, and, like a lot of geniuses, he behaves in his own way. I was pleased he chose to stay at Manchester United. He has great talent and if he has learnt from his hot-headed episode, he can definitely reach the perfection that he and Man. Utd. are after.

I enjoyed being on Jimmy Hill's *This Is Your Life*. There is one thing about Jimmy: if he does anything, then he has to be the best at it. Halfway through the programme his Boy's Brigade came on. They were all between sixty and seventy, and one of the guys had a trumpet and handed it to Jim. I knew that if he took it and played, then he would be very good, because he just wouldn't do it if he could only half play it. And he was very good.

I have a story to tell that just sums him up. We had an ex-England versus ex-Northern Ireland match in Belfast. Johnny Haynes and Jimmy Greaves were playing and Jimmy Hill was involved. After the game there was a charity function. Present was a woman entertainer singing 'Old McDonald Had a Farm', and she called three of us out to be the animals. She said to Johnny Haynes, 'You be a donkey,' then to Jimmy, 'You be the duck,' and to me, 'You be the dog.' As soon as Jimmy knew he was going to be a duck, he started frowning and was obviously very concerned. He came up to me and said, extremely seriously, 'You be the duck, because I do a great dog.' Johnny and I just fell about laughing. For us it was a bit of a joke, but for Jimmy it was deadly serious. Even in 'McDonald's Farm' he had to be the best animal. We haven't let him forget that!

Back to football tactics, and I have say that I greatly enjoyed the 1995 Coca-Cola Cup final. It was a great example of two different systems played extremely well. Bolton played the traditional 4-4-2 and Liverpool played a wonderfully entertaining game with three central defenders and the full-backs pushed in. Redknapp and Barnes were in the centre of the field, with Fowler and Rush up front.

I think that Liverpool were marginally the best team on the day. McManaman's goals were excellent examples of the type of goal he scores, but I thought Bolton's goal, a volley from Alan Thompson, was the best.

## Drugs, alcohol and football

Just as I was considering how to get the FA involved with an initiative aimed at persuading youngsters away from drugs, Paul Merson's problems came to light. The FA took very positive action. Personally, I have to say that I don't think their subsequent campaign should be limited to football. The title is 'Fit for Football'; I think that should be 'Fit for Life'. Everyone should be aware of the dangers of drugs and excessive alcohol, and how they can screw up your whole life, not just your ability to play sport.

However, the FA will invest more than a million pounds during the next five years in driving home the message, to nine-year-olds and upwards, that drugs and excessive alcohol are bad for you. Paul Merson has shown that drugs and alcohol addiction can be beaten, and he has my full support and admiration. It isn't easy to control an addiction, it takes guts and courage to admit it publicly, and then confront it and overcome it. He will need support for the rest of his life, but I am sure that if he has come this far then he will continue to be a good example of what can be done if you have the right attitude. Again, like Gazza, this is something he can never be complacent about, that same self-destruct button is always there. I hope things go well for him.

For my part, I will continue to hassle major companies and try to get them to start investing in our youth. I want them to build pitches and provide amenities. It is criminal that a lot of our playing fields have been sold off. A few teachers came to see me in my office at the FA, and one teacher who teaches at a school in Canary Wharf, in London's Docklands, has to organize a coach for his kids to go to Enfield (north London) to play football for an hour! It's just crazy and against all my instincts of what is right for kids. We do need to get this sorted out, and the Government has to help schools to provide the right facilities. It's easy to produce documents, but we need hard cash to ensure our children grow up with a healthy attitude and to ensure football is an important part of the twenty-first century.

# CHAPTER THIRTEEN

## THE ORGANIZATION: EURO 96 UPDATE

Back in April 1995, Glen Kirton was in an optimistic mood about Euro 96. He reported that the league clubs were still in negotiation with ISL Marketing, the company that bought the entire sponsorship rights for the Championship from UEFA. So there was no definite agreement on that front, but there had been a pitch inspection. UEFA's stadium committee, chaired by Scot Ernie Walker, had been over to see if our stadiums were in full working order, and whether any needed updating. The stadiums far surpassed expectations. Ernie Walker said that, 'In terms of general standard, presentation, public services, seating, the dressing rooms and facilities for the media, England have the best grounds in the world.'

This is very comforting for England and a big feather in our caps. Everyone moans about the state of English football, but it seems that we have got something right. Walker also said, 'It was very gratifying to come back, almost two years after the first inspection, and find that all the original promises had been kept.'

I don't think we should underestimate this comment. We should be proud of the fact that we have taken things seriously. Other countries involved in World Cups and European Championship finals have had enormous delays in finalizing the necessary alterations to their stadiums. We were ready almost a year early. The Taylor Report undoubtedly helped. As Glen says: 'We may not be able to claim credit for the vision required to put these changes into place, but English football can claim credit for the way it has responded to the report and its recommendations.'

Glen is adamant that security is already in place, and there will be a very sophisticated ticketing system. With regards to Dublin, Glen insists it couldn't happen here. We have more control over the distribution of tickets and the security involved in policing the fans. 'The riot actually involved a very small number of so-called fans. There are more people involved in animal rights demonstrations than in football hooliganism.'

Euro 96 now had more staff. As well as Glen and deputy director Adrian Titcombe, there are four managers for the eight stadiums, which have been divided into four centres, and a variety of marketing and media personnel.

Preparations for the Umbro summer tournament were also going very well. Fifty thousand tickets had been sold by the end of April, for six games, with an average capacity of 45,000 each game.

# CHAPTER FOURTEEN

## TOWARDS THE SUMMER TOURNAMENT

Unsurprisingly, my end of April get-together attracted criticism from the Press. Some journalists, like Brian Glanville and John Sadler, criticized me for disrupting the Premier League. These guys really should know better. It was an international week. Even if I hadn't got the squad together, the Premier League would have been suspended due to the fact that Scotland, Holland, Sweden, Ireland and Germany were playing, and so all the players from these countries would have had to be released from their clubs anyway.

I wanted to bring some new faces in, players who may be involved in the future. It gave me the opportunity to look at things in the long term, and start looking at a hard core of World Cup players who will be ready in 1998.

One new addition to our team was Mike Kelly, whom I brought in as goalkeeping coach. He had been involved with England during Bobby Robson's time, but not during Graham Taylor's. I think he is outstanding. I wanted the best to work with the best. The work he was doing with Seaman, Flowers, James and Walker was innovative.

During the couple of days we had together we did some work on interchanging positions. I need players to be able to rotate around the positions if there is an injury or if we need to change our tactical play. I already knew that Anderton, Gazza and Platt could do this, but I wanted the others to practise it. I thought this would be beneficial for everyone, as when the new players come into the team they will then already know what I am looking for.

The chance to work together like this cuts down the time needed to get to know one another and discover what players can do, and is what is needed in the team.

I would very much like to have more of these get-togethers as we approach the European Championship finals. I'd also like to see them held in different parts of the country, so that the local Press can get to know us and talk about England. We were in Birmingham in April 1995, and that provided a chance to meet the West Midlands Press and start to build up a rapport for the finals. Villa Park is a venue for the European Championship, and it's important we start to get to see media faces who will be following us, or other teams, during those matches.

It is also a chance for the local fans to see us. I believe that the England team should be seen around the country; after all, it is the England team, not the London team. In Italy, they play their national games around the country in the various stadiums, from Palermo to Udine, and I think this is important for building up national loyalty. It is difficult to get really involved in a team if you only see them on the telly.

This time, the Press were very interested in the presence of Stan Collymore, who was in the squad for the first time. Certain sections of the media had been pressing for his inclusion, and they weren't disappointed. I was very pleased with his performance during the training matches. I thought he put on a good show. Cole, although he had a bit of a knock, also looked very sharp. Mark Draper, then of Leicester City, attracted interest, as he is quite local to Birmingham. He did well too.

So all in all, despite the harping from the Press, we made good progress. I sometimes wonder if some members of the tabloids want us to do well next year, or whether they would rather have some sensationalist headlines.

## Gascoigne

I don't think there has ever been a player who has attracted as much comment as Gazza. I decided to go down to watch his return at the Olympic Stadium. I knew he was going to play, but I didn't know for how long. It turned out that he played the full ninety minutes.

Lazio invited me into the dressing room before the game. Gazza was very excited to be playing after a year out of football.

He couldn't wait to start. And when he ran on to the pitch the cheers reverberated around the Olympic Stadium. There is no doubt that he is a much-loved personality, and it is to the credit of the fans that they have been patient during all his injuries.

He certainly hasn't lost his nerve. Although he wasn't trying to get stuck into people himself, he put himself into positions where he could have been hit; he wasn't holding back and trying to protect himself. He was running at defenders with the ball as he always has done. There were glimpses of his old trade mark, the famous dribbling passages through defence. With a bit more luck, he could have scored. In fact he should have scored. He'd also lost an enormous amount of weight over the preceding months; three stone in total! He was looking slimmer than I'd ever seen him. He was working out three times a day, and then working out in the gym in the evening. Even his mate Jimmy had lost two stone and was no longer 'five bellies'!

## Postcard from Spain (May 1995)

Yvette and I managed to get away for a few days with Bobby and Jan Keetch. Bobby used to play for Fulham, but then he became a gourmet and decided travelling round the world sampling local delights was better than running up and down a wet and windy pitch. Sometimes, I wish I'd made the same decision.

We went off to Majorca to a small place called Deia on the north west of the island. It was just fantastic: the weather was great and Toots managed really to get back on the road to recovery after her knee operation. She has had the problem for some years. If she moved sharply the knee would dislocate itself. Finally it got to the point where the surgeon operated. In Majorca she could get in the pool everyday and do exercises and help build up the muscles.

From my point of view I used the time to get my mind clear about the summer Umbro tournament. I thought about systems and individual players, and what to do if certain key players weren't available. For example, I mulled over the likely problem of what I would do if Tony Adams dropped out through injury. I had expected to lose a centre-half in Neil Ruddock through injury, but that left John Scales, Pallister, Howey and Adams. Then Howey dropped out, followed, while I was in Spain, by Adams. Sitting on my balcony and looking at the beautiful blue sea, I thought of

David Unsworth and three more players who could cover several positions: Colin Cooper of Nottingham Forest, Richard Shaw and Gareth Southgate, then of Crystal Palace.

# CHAPTER FIFTEEN

## THE SEASON ENDS AND THE SUMMER TOURNAMENT BEGINS

### The League Championship

I really think that 1995 saw one of the most exciting finals to any season. Blackburn were way ahead at one point and then Manchester United clawed their way back into contention. The run-in had so many twists and turns, it was like something out of an Agatha Christie novel. And what a dramatic last day. Blackburn's manager Kenny Dalgleish was back at his old club Liverpool, and Manchester United were down in London at Upton Park.

United had to beat West Ham, so it was really all down to them. I watched it on the television at home, and I have to say that it was football coverage at its best. Sky Sports had a split screen between the matches so you could watch them simultaneously; the marriage between the Premier League and Sky television has been a very successful one as long as you have a satellite dish. Personally, I would like to see football reach the largest audience possible on either BBC or ITV.

The game culminated in a really stunning last half-hour, but Manchester United's failure to beat West Ham meant Blackburn hung on to be crowned Champions despite losing at Liverpool.

I think that a good end to the season did help to restore the image of the Premier League. After all the problems during the winter, it was as though we were heralding the dawn of a new era and going back to playing attractive football on the pitch, with no sordid occurrences behind the scenes. In that finale we really had a glimpse of what is great about the English game, and why other countries try and emulate our style and passion.

Throughout the season I had been impressed by Jürgen Klinsmann. He is a great ambassador for Germany and did a good job for Tottenham. It was a shame and, in fact, completely unnecessary that it ended on a sour note. I met Jürgen in the VIP room before the Football Writers' dinner where he was voted Footballer of the Year. We talked about some of the Tottenham players. He said he thought Teddy Sheringham was outstanding and that Sol Campbell could be one of the best full-backs in Europe. He then went on to say that he was very disappointed that the situation regarding his contract hadn't been made clear. He had never had a get-out option. His had been a one-year-plus-one contract; so effectively it was a one-year contract.

Jürgen was very disillusioned, believing that some at Tottenham had tried to manipulate the crowd against him and hide the truth. Of course I have never experienced this type of problem! But the crowd didn't turn against him – they appreciated what he had done for them, and I think that from the fans' point of view it is better to have loved and lost him than never to have loved him at all.

However, Klinsmann's type of move creates problems from several angles. Firstly, I believe that the fans should be treated with respect, and deserve to know the truth. Secondly, it creates a false economy. If you bring in a player like Klinsmann, even if it is for a short time, you have to pay him a lot of money. So say, for example, he's on £20,000 a week, this creates unrest amongst the other members of the team, who say, 'Hang on a minute, I'm not as good as him, but I'm worth at least half of that.' So then you have to give the other players pay rises, and when the star leaves (particularly if he only stays for a short time), you're still left with an inflated pay roll.

### The FA Cup Final

I always thought it would be tight with Everton not allowing Manchester United the space to play in, and it turned out just like that. It wasn't a classic match, but I thought that Everton deserved it on the day.

### Paul Gascoigne (yet again)

It is difficult to keep Gazza out of the headlines, and no sooner had I landed back in London after having gone to watch him play his comeback match for Lazio in Rome than rumours started about a move back to England. The Press tried to imply that I was advising him to choose an English club rather than Glasgow Rangers, but this was not true. I did not act as a mediator in any deals or try to influence him one way or the other. The main thing is for him to be happy and I'm sure he'll enjoy being with a big club like Rangers, who can also offer him a chance to play in Europe in the Champions' Cup.

I think Gazza liked Walter Smith, the manager of Rangers, and I'm fairly sure he wasn't that keen about the other offers on the table, so he decided on Glasgow. I don't think he'll find it quite as demanding as playing in England, as there are just three or four top clubs in Scotland. This means there won't be the same week-in, week-out pressure of having to play at a consistently high level. Scottish Premier League clubs can play each other four or five times in a season with cup matches and so they get to know each other pretty well. It isn't the same as having to live life in the gold fish bowl of the Premier League.

I read Andrew Longmore's profile of Gazza in *The Times* at the beginning of June and I particularly agreed with Longmore's conclusion that 'Gascoigne's football says more about the man than any amount of psychoanalysis. The joy, the freedom, the exuberance, the craziness, the crudity. It is all right there on the field . . . whatever else has changed in his life, Gascoigne's love of football has not. He still plays expecting to see coats on the ground instead of goalposts.' Ron Greenwood's analogy is that the perfect player would be an extrovert on the pitch and an introvert off it. I agree with this. You want a player who can express himself freely on the pitch, but contain himself off it.

**The summer tournament**
Finally, the moment when our first real test comes, but it threatens to be somewhat of a shallow test, as a lot of my key players are injured.

I went into the three games against Japan, Sweden and Brazil without players like Seaman, Jones, Lee Dixon, Ruddock, Howey, Adams, Tim Sherwood, Wise, Venison and Ince. The list just got longer and longer. I suppose that's the price I pay as England Coach for having an important tournament at the end of a very long and demanding league season. It will be the same for Euro 96.

## The Squad
Tim Flowers – Blackburn Rovers
Ian Walker – Tottenham Hotspur
Warren Barton – Wimbledon
Gary Neville – Manchester United
David Unsworth – Everton
Gary Pallister – Manchester United
John Scales – Liverpool
Graeme Le Saux – Blackburn Rovers
Stuart Pearce – Nottingham Forest
Darren Anderton – Tottenham Hotspur
David Batty – Blackburn Rovers
David Platt – Sampdoria
Jamie Redknapp – Liverpool
Paul Gascoigne – Lazio
John Barnes – Liverpool
Steve McManaman – Liverpool
Nick Barmby – Tottenham Hotspur
Peter Beardsley – Newcastle United
Alan Shearer – Blackburn Rovers
Stan Collymore – Nottingham Forest
Colin Cooper – Nottingham Forest
Teddy Sheringham – Tottenham Hotspur

As we had three games in eight days I was prepared for the fact that probably none of the players would feature in all three games. Captain Platt and I had a little chat and I told him that it was my aim to rest some of the players, but on the other hand I wondered if this was entirely realistic, bearing in mind that so many of the regular England players were injured. This was particularly true in defence, where there were a glut of new caps.

Our opponents in the Umbro Tournament were:

**Japan** who have fast become a soccer-mad nation. They have imported some of the best talent in the world into the J league. The Italian player Daniele Massaro, who has done so well for AC Milan, is about to go to Japan. Then of course our own Gary Lineker went out there for a couple of years. These imports are providing excellent role models from which home-grown talent can learn their craft. And it has to be said that Japanese players are improving all the time. I was not expecting this side to be a pushover at all.

**Sweden** who are one of the top teams in Europe. They finished third in the 1994 World Cup, and are a very attractive side. They manage to combine organization, discipline and a direct game, with flare and skill. Martin Dahlin, Tomas Brolin and Janos Thern are outstanding players who all have individual flair and talent. However, their big strength is that they manage to keep disciplined and I think that combination of skill and discipline is what got them so far in the last World Cup.

**Brazil** who are the current World Champions. They had to wait twenty-four years to regain their status as the best team in the world, and, as I keep saying, I think that is down to bringing organization into their game.

I have found two major differences in managing the national team from managing a club side, and these differences have caused problems. I think one of the most vital aspects of successful club management is the ability to communicate well. As a manager or coach you have to be able to sit down with a player, or players, and discuss how they are contributing to the game, and what you expect from them. To play to their best the players need to have 100 per cent confidence in the manager, and to get this they have to understand why they cannot always be sure of a first-team place. With the England team, if I want to rest a first-choice player so that I can have a look at one of the fringe players, I often have to speak to the first-choice player on the phone rather than sit down with him. I find this very difficult: the phone is such a cold method of communication. It can easily lead to misunderstandings, and you can't afford to have any of those. There are enough pressures without unnecessary ones creeping into the picture.

The other problem is that of players leaving straight after the match and then not having a chance to analyse the game until our next meeting. Unfortunately, I have no option but to keep it this way – I am busy with the media for at least two hours after a game, and I can't expect the players to sit in the dressing-room until well after midnight. The alternative is to ignore the demands of the media, and if I feel it is in the best interests of the team after one particular match to sit down and talk it through, then I do so.

## The summer tournament training camp

Dave Butler and Alan Smith, our two talented physios, are like Siamese twins; they do everything together and share the same status and responsibilities. They are both equally important to the smooth running of the team and without them things would soon come to a grinding halt.

Alan and Dave work on the pitch morning and afternoon with the injured players, although, as I've said, if there is any doubt about a player regaining his fitness in time for the match, he is released to go back to his club. The club always comes first.

I am obviously in constant contact with the club managers regarding any of their players who are injured. Some managers are happy for their players to stay with us and be treated, while some like them straight back with the club. Roy Evans of Liverpool, for instance, is very co-operative and thinks it is beneficial for his injured players to be with us. Our cut-off point in deciding whether players will make it or not is the Saturday before the match on Wednesday.

Alan and Dave arrive before the rest of the squad. They set up a medical room which consists of two beds, a shortwave machine and an ultrasonic machine and all manner of lotions and potions. Michelle Rogers, our international secretary, informs Dave and Alan about the various injuries before the players arrive. They also lay out three sets of training kit for each player. The first kit is for the first training session, the other one is for the following day.

Normally the players get up at about eight forty-five in the morning, but the injured players get up earlier so they can have treatment before we go to the training ground. Once we are at the training ground, Don, Bryan or Dave do the warm up, which consists of twenty minutes' jogging and stretching, while the injured players will either do this or just walk. Treatments can take place in the morning, afternoon and early evening, and this is the time when the fit players have massages and then swim or sit in the jacuzzi.

At the end of the session, we all troop off to the canteen to have a cup of coffee. Dave and Alan will collect the balls and bibs and load them on to the coach.

We all eat at seven or seven-thirty, and then the evenings are free for the players. They chuck their kit out of their rooms and leave it lying in the corridor, where it is collected by the staff from the hotel and then whisked off to the hotel laundry.

There is a light training session on match day, and a few minor treatments as everyone should be fit by then. The players give their football boots to Dave and Alan by lunchtime on match day. We make them sign their names to say they've given them to us, so we know if there are any missing boots!

While the players are resting, Dave and Alan start their journey to the match venue. Having cleaned the boots they then leave with a minibus stacked high with four big cases, plus the doctor's bag and eight big sacks full of kit and physio's equipment.

Dave and Alan should arrive at the ground at about four o'clock and start setting up the dressing room. When we are away, the host nation will often do the setting up for us. The Irish did everything for us at Lansdowne Road – not that we, or rather a certain section of the crowd, thanked them in the best manner possible.

Dave and Alan are always keen to get everything right so we don't arrive with some of the kit missing. We did this once in Scotland; England forgot the goalkeeper's jerseys and Peter Shilton had to wear the Scottish goalkeeper's shirt.

Nowadays it is more organized than the Army. The match kit is always arranged in the same order with the shirt as the last item to be placed on top. The player's names are pinned on the wall with a list of their sizes, so the right kit is given to the right player, and in theory nothing should go wrong.

I always make sure there is a blackboard in the dressing room so that I can go over a few tactical points if necessary. While I'm chatting to the players, Dave and Allen take the sponsors' boxes which sit by the bench and will promote the names associated with the FA to the crowd. They also take out a spare bag full of shorts, studs, surgical collars, ice packs and other equipment and leave it near the bench. Dave and Alan divide their time absolutely equally. If there is an injury, whoever ran on first the last time will run on second this time.

Both Alan and Dave say they love the job of working with England, although it is a bit frustrating to lose the day-to-day touch with the players that you have in club football. Physios are like doctors; they like to follow the progress of injuries and see how the players respond to treatment. I worked with Dave at QPR, Crystal Palace and Tottenham, and I think that both he and Alan are doing an excellent job for England.

Tactically I have never been far away from either the Christmas tree formation or the diamond. I was confident that if things didn't work out we could easily return to this style of play. When I was originally thinking about the Umbro tournament I decided to experiment with the back four. We hadn't conceded many goals and I thought we needed to push either a centre-half or a full-back into midfield to prevent being outnumbered in that area.

However, when I heard that Adams, Ruddock, Howey and Pallister were all unfit, I knew that I couldn't experiment tactically as it would be unfair to ask the new caps to do something different from what they had been used to doing for their clubs. But it wasn't all negative; on the plus side I was able to see new players who were perhaps ahead of their time gaining a place in the first team, who would give me a good idea of what they were capable of.

This was our first opportunity to play against Japan. As we all know, Japan is a new nation as far as interest in football is concerned, but they are investing a lot of money and time into the development of the game. As they are so new to the game, there aren't many videos or other forms of tangible evidence of their performances so far, so it is difficult to comment on individuals, but Kazuyoshi Miura is one of the better-known players. He is a centre-forward who, although born in Japan, has had experience in Brazil and then with the Italian club Genoa. Although he had been sidelined through injury I was expecting him to make quite an impression.

The most revolutionary changes to our side came in defence, in which there were three new caps: Gary Neville, the Manchester United right-back; David Unsworth who, although only 21, was already an FA Cup winner with Everton; and John Scales also at centre-half. Stuart Pearce was brought in alongside them as an experienced hand.

However, what had the Press on red alert was the debut of Stan Collymore. At the time I thought Stan was ready for England, but that the Press were putting unnecessary pressure on him. Playing for England for the first time is an awesome experience in itself, and the players can do without the added stress of overly high expectations. Headlines like the one in the *Daily Mail* on Saturday 3 June ('Collymore in shop window') don't, in my mind, help the player or the team. He knew what was expected of him and he set out to do his best. He didn't need to be terrified into thinking everything hinged on his single performance.

The same applied to Paul Gascoigne. The fact that he was on the substitutes' bench did not in anyway indicate he would remain there for longer than necessary. I fielded a team I felt was the best for the game against Japan, bearing in mind that fourteen regular international players were not available due to injury.

ENGLAND V JAPAN 3 June 1995
Wembley stadium
Attendance: 21,142
England: Flowers, Neville, Scales, Unsworth, Pearce, Anderton, Batty (Gascoigne 68), Platt, Beardsley (McManaman 68), Shearer, Collymore (Sheringham 77)
Japan: Maekawa, Tasaka, Hashiratani, Ihara, Narahashi, Morishima (Fukuda 81), Yamaguchi, Kitazawa, Soma (Yanagimoto 74), Miura, Nakayama (Kurosaki 65)
Result: 2–1
Scorers: Anderton 48, Platt 87 (pen)
         Ihara 62
Sent off: Hashiratani 87 (handling the ball in the goal area)
Referee: J Uilenberg (Holland)

In spite of all the protestations, we did win, although I am the first to admit that it wasn't a classic match. I would like to emphasize the fact that there wasn't one defender in the back four who had played in my previous internationals. The defence played well until they became a little spread out in the last twenty minutes. I thought that it was vitally important that the three new caps had the experience of Stuart Pearce, whom they could count on for guidance. In training, Stan Collymore had looked good up front with Alan Shearer, and I decided that he was ready to make his debut against Japan at Wembley. But like many players before him he froze and didn't do himself justice. I played a 'split' striker system with Shearer in front of Collymore, which Collymore is doing now at Liverpool, coming from deeper and running at the defence. But as Collymore reverted to a more traditional position

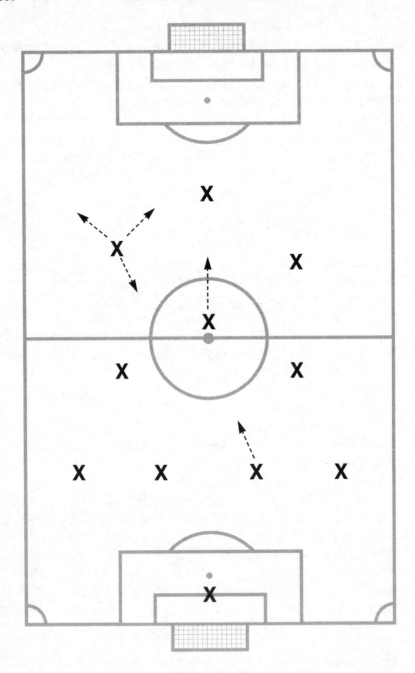

**England's formation versus Japan**

◄---- Shows player movement

playing alongside Shearer, we had to adapt. During the half-time interval I asked Shearer to drop back deeper as the midfield were finding it difficult to support the strikers. He did this and Collymore stayed in the position he felt comfortable in; and it worked better. By the Press comments you'd think there had been another Pearl Harbour, but we had beaten them and without the chance to put the new tactical system into play. The young players had had to pick up what they could, as there hadn't been the time to mould them into the team.

Considering the circumstances, I felt quietly confident at the way things had gone. However, I arrived home and found another inquisition! Toots never usually comments on the matches, apart from saying 'well done' or 'tough luck'. But as I opened the door she said, 'Why didn't you play Gazza on earlier?' I couldn't believe it, it was like walking into a press conference. I love my wife and I know she always has my best interests at heart, but I didn't feel like justifying my decisions yet again! I just said, 'Don't you start,' and went upstairs to lie down. I'll let Toots take over the story:

Terry wasn't in the best of moods when he arrived home; it had been a demanding and exhausting start for him. Anyway, he went and lay down, and I carried on getting ready to go to Scribes. Suddenly, I was aware of this scratching sound. I said, 'What are you doing?' He just said, 'Nothing,' but it still continued, and then I realized what it was. 'You're scratching your tactics on the pillow, aren't you?' I said. He looked a bit sheepish and said, 'Yes'. And there he was, scratching the pillow with his fingernail, still so involved in the match that he was going through all the moves. He has the most incredible photographic memory. Sometimes we'll be watching a video of one of the England matches, and he'll say watch what so and so does next, and sure enough they'll do exactly what he said. Anyway, after a rest, he was back to normal and we went off to Scribes to spend a pleasant evening with friends.

Even though the Swedes were without their World Cup stars Brolin, Dahlin, Limpar, Schwarz, Blomqvist and Rehn, they were still a formidable side.

I was delighted to be playing our first home game at Elland Road. We travelled to Leeds, and stayed at the Oulton Hall Hotel.

The morning after we arrived we had a meeting to discuss the match against Japan. I told the players what I thought about their performances – the defence played well and the midfield needed to make sure they still provided adequate service. The main objective of the meeting was to get a greater input from the squad. We achieved that, and I sensed a new desire from them to be forthcoming and also to accept criticism, which is important if progress is to be made. I was very happy with the players' attitude and we went on to discuss the match against Sweden.

I set out a positive attacking game plan without making it too complicated, which is something I am always aware of. I made a few changes. Warren Barton came in for Neville. Barton had only appeared once for England (for the 27 minutes against the Republic of Ireland). He is a very promising full-back. My only concern was that he was then playing in midfield (rather than defence) for Wimbledon. I also brought in Colin Cooper, the Nottingham Forest defender as a new cap. I kept Flowers in goal as he had put in a good performance against Japan and in previous games. I gambled on Pallister's injury. I thought that maybe it would be important for him to play, even if he wasn't fully fit. And I was keen to try Le Saux back in instead of Pearce. I had a midfield of Anderton, Platt, Barnes and Beardsley.

I decided to bring John Barnes back into the team to play a similar role to the one he has at Liverpool; that is to concentrate on his skills in passing the ball and to develop patiently the game by acting as a central pivotal force so that others can create opportunities by playing off him.

I thought this would be important for creating enough attacking opportunities to ensure our strikers, Alan Shearer and Teddy Sheringham, were getting good service. A lot has been said about two strikers as opposed to one.

We were very successful in the 1990 World Cup with Lineker and Beardsley in a split striker formation, with Beardsley playing deeper and left of the box, leaving ideal space for Gary. In recent years we have reverted to two strikers up front and we haven't got the results. The facts also demonstrate that in the last World Cup seventeen teams out of twenty-four played with split centre-forwards. The underrated Sheringham is the one who can play in both formations. He can play up front and also drop deeper.

I was hoping that Shearer, Platt, Anderton and Flowers would play in all three games – injuries permitting. There seemed to be no problems with Flowers. Platt was at the end of the Italian season, which isn't as aggressive as the English season. Platt is also very fit, but he had suffered from a knee injury, which I thought he might still be carrying. Although he wasn't misleading me in any way, he is very dedicated to playing for England and I know it means a lot to him to lead the side out and provide on-pitch encouragement and instruction.

I thought it might be more difficult for Anderton and Shearer to make all three games. Shearer had experienced the emotion and exhaustion of winning the league title, and after a long season Anderton had then played in China and not had any rest at all. I was expecting them to be doubtful for the Brazil game.

ENGLAND V SWEDEN 8 June 1995
Elland Road
Attendance: 32,008
England: Flowers, Barton, Le Saux, Cooper, Pallister (Scales 80), Anderton, Platt, Shearer, Beardsley (Barmby 64), Barnes (Gascoigne 64), Sheringham
Sweden: Ravelli, Sundgrun, Lucic, Bjorklund, Kamark, Alexandersson, Mild, Erlingmark (O Andersson 89), Gudmundsson, K Andersson (Lidman 84), Larsson
Result: 3–3
Scorers: Sheringham 44, Platt 89, Anderton 90
        Mild 11, 37, Andersson 46
Referee: L Mottram (Scotland)

I thought this was one of the most exciting England matches for a long time. Sweden surprised us with their compact, attacking style and got two goals past us before we got a grip of things. We made some very unnecessary defensive errors. I am not going to defend these; we just have to learn and do better in the future. The second and third goals that the Swedes scored simply should not have been allowed to happen, but they did, and it was to our credit that, instead of letting our heads drop and giving up, we rose to the challenge and, exhibiting true British grit, fought right to the bitter end.

Kennet Andersson is a player I admire very much and he amply demonstrated his high level of skill and his opportunist touch.

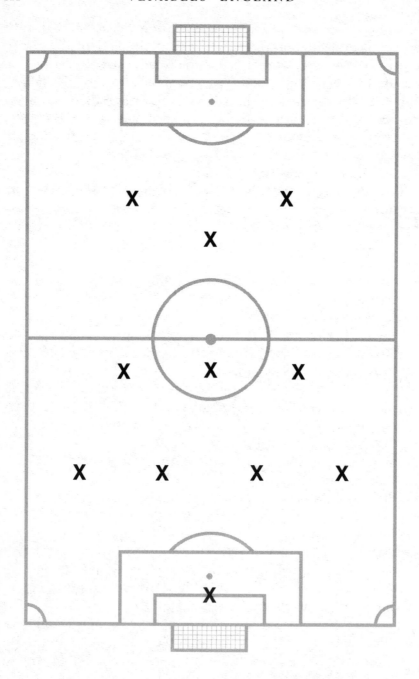

**England's formation versus USA, Sweden and Portugal**

In addition to the split strikers, Platt played further forward, and scored. Generally our attacking play was much better than our defensive play. We should not have been 3–1 down with everything to play for in the last five minutes. However, on the plus side we proved that our fitness was good, and the team spirit and attacking flair was even better. You can't fight back against a team like Sweden if you don't have those ingredients. I was pleased with midfield and attack at the end of the game. Now we had to tighten up the defence for the last match, against the World Champions, Brazil.

# CHAPTER SIXTEEN

## THE WORLD CHAMPIONS COME TO WEMBLEY

I was very excited about the prospect of playing against Brazil. A lot of rubbish had been written about the team lacking its stars, Romario and Bebeto, and coming to England as an 'ordinary' side. Well, I can tell you that no Brazilian side is ever ordinary, and never will be.

You only have to watch these kids playing on the beaches and in the streets, as I have done, to stand back and marvel at the level of natural skill. Usually, the only things these street teams lack are organization and discipline, and as we have already discussed, this is what the last Brazilian coach, Carlos Alberto Parreira, instilled in the team that went on to win the 1994 World Cup. When you harness a high level of natural skill with the ability to think and plan ahead, then you get a world-beating team.

ENGLAND V BRAZIL 10 June 1995
Wembley stadium
Attendance: 67,318
England: Flowers, Neville, Scales (Barton 90), Cooper, Pearce, Anderton, Batty (Gascoigne 79), Platt, Le Saux, Shearer, Sheringham (Collymore 79)
Brazil: Zetti, Jorginho, Aldair (Ronaldao 90), Marcio Santos, Sampaio, Roberto Carlos, Edmundo, Dunga, Ronaldo (Giovanni 76), Juninho (Leonardo 84), Zinho
Result: 1–3
Scorers: Le Saux 38
         Juninho 53, Ronaldo 60, Edmundo 75

Referee: P Luigi Pairetto (Italy).

The atmosphere at Wembley was electric. The England rugby team had just beaten Australia in the quarter-finals of the Rugby World Cup, and the crowd burst into a spontaneous rendition of the England team anthem 'Swing Low Sweet Chariot' as we walked out on to the pitch.

It was another grey old drizzly day, but we were all looking forward to playing the World Champions. There is nothing like a big match to fill the heart with hope and enthusiasm, and the reaction of the fans as we lined up for the national anthems was very uplifting. The President of FIFA, the Brazilian João Havelange, was at Wembley to hand over the Umbro Cup to the winners of the tournament.

We got off to a very good start. I was particularly pleased with the way we communicated and gelled together from the offset. Darren Anderton kept Roberto Carlos under control very well. It was his job to keep close to the Brazilian, but I didn't want Anderton just to run with him, I wanted Roberto Carlos to chase him.

Graeme Le Saux played further forward than he normally does, and this gave us better balance on the left; and in fact the team was better balanced overall. Le Saux's job was to stiffen up the midfield and get wide for the crosses. I said to him, 'It's no different to what you are used to. You just have to play a bit further forward, from where you can make twice the number of runs than from your normal position at the back.' Sheringham was going to stop the ball going to their right-back Jorginho, and once it was over the halfway line then he was Le Saux's responsibility, freeing Teddy to jog into the centre to make the split centre-forward effect.

David Platt worked hard to fill the midfield with David Batty, and make his forward runs when possible. Up until half-time it all went very well. We scored through Le Saux and we should have had a penalty. Teddy Sheringham was fouled when it looked like he was going to score. I really think that for forty-five minutes we had them rattled: we looked like the better side. There were excellent signs of a good side emerging from this. I would question the judgement of anyone who said otherwise.

We then gave a silly free-kick away on the edge of the box and

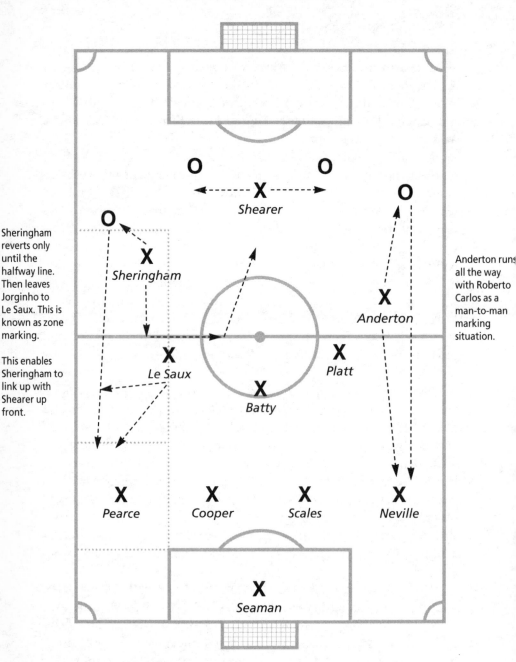

Sheringham reverts only until the halfway line. Then leaves Jorginho to Le Saux. This is known as zone marking.

This enables Sheringham to link up with Shearer up front.

Anderton runs all the way with Roberto Carlos as a man-to-man marking situation.

O

X
Shearer

O

O

X
Sheringham

X
Anderton

X
Le Saux

X
Platt

X
Batty

X
Pearce

X
Cooper

X
Scales

X
Neville

X
Seaman

**England's formation during play versus Brazil**
*showing zone marking and man-to-man marking*

◀----  Shows player movement

they scored. I think we took this too hard and started to fall to pieces. The players' worst fears had been realized and we began to give them too much respect. We slumped until Gazza and Collymore came on. Collymore looked a lot more comfortable in this match and did himself justice after his first cap against Japan.

This was a classy Brazilian side. Their manager Mario Zagalo said that for the next five years Brazil will rule the game. For the manager to make that claim he is putting himself under tremendous pressure, and I don't think he would do that if he couldn't also keep to his word. Juninho was incredible; if anything they looked an even better side than the one that won the World Cup.

Overall, I was pleased that we took the initiative and scored, but we have to learn to sustain it for ninety minutes and, weathering the storms along the way, come back again rather than slump. We learnt from this game, and by now one of my main objectives had almost been achieved, namely that no player should be an automatic choice for the team. I wanted us to go into Euro 96 with at least two players for every position. No player should feel that he is the only one for the job; I want the players hungry and willing to learn at each step.

I think that the new caps learnt a lot through the tournament. We had a few defensive problems during the Sweden match, but considering that four or five of our first choice centre-halves were out, the new players adapted well. We discussed the situation afterwards and made repairs for the last match against Brazil. I think we showed that our attack was very strong, particularly during the Sweden match. Individually, I was very pleased with Neville. Redknapp and McManaman didn't get much of a chance to play, but they seemed to become involved with the squad and pick up things in training quickly. I think it was very valuable experience for them.

I was pleased with the progress overall, but more fine-tuning is needed before the European Championship finals. My only complaint at this point was the same one I had when I became England Coach, and that is that we were still scrabbling around for games.

# Chapter Seventeen

## The Bunker

To handle all my non-FA business I have a private office, which is run by my close friend and confidant, Eddie Ashby. Eddie and I have been through thick and thin together since he started to run my affairs several years ago. Eddie was my personal assistant at Tottenham Hotspur when I was Chief Executive, and he has been my right-hand man in the fight for unfair dismissal from Tottenham Hotspur against Alan Sugar. Eddie is one of my most trusted advisers and has the type of meticulous mind that keeps every single piece of paper pertaining to all my business affairs.

Eddie is the main man who deals with all my legal affairs and he liaises with my solicitor, Nick Trainer. Eddie is the person who provides information for the barristers and other legal people who represent me in my various legal battles. Most large companies employ a team of expert legal eagles to advise them, but Eddie has handled everything on his own. Eddie and Nick spearhead my legal battles. They work alongside two other companies: Clifford Chance, who are working on the libel case that Alan Sugar is bringing against me from my autobiography; and Burton Copeland, who are working for me on the DTI case.

Eddie also oversees some of my longer-term business interests. Essentially, these are the private members' club Scribes, which is largely run by my wife, and the media-related promotional activity that my high profile generates; for example I am involved with Green Flag, the main sponsors of the England team, and also with Mars, Umbro and ITV. All the day-to-day administration of my affairs I leave to Eddie and his small team, which consists of our full-time secretary Beata, our bookkeeper Yola and operations manager Joe.

I'd like to answer the question that so many people ask: 'As you have the England job, why continue to sue various people and companies? Why not just accept what you have and let it all die down?'

Well, I have to say that it is a point of principle. I was brought up to believe that if you did something wrong you were punished, and if you were right you fought on until it was proved you were right. And that is exactly what I am doing. I gave my trust to people who, the way I see things, have betrayed it, and my strong sense of integrity has been compromised by unfair accusations which have not only been bandied about in the press but have also been the subject of several court cases.

For the sake of my family I have to carry on and prove I am right. I don't think any of you would give up what you know is rightfully yours. I have to defend a reputation I built up over thirty-five years, and which was unfairly destroyed in the thirty-five minutes it took for *Panorama* to broadcast their first programme in 1993. They then broadcast another negative documentary on me in 1994. It is unprecedented that someone should have two major investigative programmes dedicated to them within the space of a year. Even really high-profile people like Gerry Adams haven't had a look in yet, and Princess Diana had to appear in person before she was granted a programme to herself. I was only a football manager and not even England Coach at the time.

At the very same time that I was appointed to the England job (late January 1994), Alan Sugar began his action to wind up my company Edennote. This was the company that owned my services in Tottenham Hotspur plc. It also had a five-year management contract which parallelled my own service contract with Tottenham.

In Autumn 1993, having given up on my efforts to remain at Tottenham and buy out Alan Sugar, I had sued for wrongful dismissal and breach of contract as the agreements had more than three years to run. In the summer of 1993, during the process of the high-profile court actions, Sugar allegedly ran up legal costs of some £450,000. This figure was never verified. An application to the court first reduced this to some £335,000 and then an interim award of a more credible £185,000.

Despite Edennote's claim against Tottenham, worth in excess of £500,000, plus its own costs of another £200,000, Sugar pushed ahead with his winding-up petition. The publicly quoted aim was to recover his legal costs. The more plausible objective, however, was that he wanted to stifle my claim; the only other material creditor in Edennote being myself, and I was owed almost £1 million.

Regrettably, and after a determined defence over some months, the court decided against me, and the company was compulsorily wound up in May 1994. The Official Receiver, having first approached myself and Sugar, appointed a liquidator to the company. His name was Stephen Ryman. Undaunted and anxious to pursue my claim I approached Mr Ryman with a view to having the right of action assigned back to me personally. Having taken legal advice and negotiated hard over the loans, Mr Ryman agreed, and my claim against Tottenham was once more under my control.

Alan Sugar was obviously infuriated and applied to the court to have Mr Ryman removed as the liquidator of Edennote. The case was heard in early November 1994, barely two days after the showing of the second *Panorama* programme about me. The timing could not have been worse if the showing had been deliberately timed to create the maximum prejudice against me. It was also only a few days before the England international against Nigeria. Our legal counsel had advised that we had a very high chance of success and, on the basis of long-established law, Sugar's task was extremely difficult. Notwithstanding, after a hearing of some five days, and to the astonishment of both Mr Ryman's counsel and my own, Mr Justice Vinelott ruled that Mr Ryman be replaced.

Such was the disbelief at this judgement that we have launched an appeal; this will be heard before the Court of Appeal in April 1996. Once again, however, here hangs a tale. My counsel have informed me that the rules of procedure in the Court of Appeal are very strict and that time constraints are equally rigid. Applications to the court have to be made within time limits or seriously risk being debarred. With this in mind, we duly lodged our appeal application well within time. Not so Mr Sugar. His application was several months out of time and he had to obtain special leave from the court. Lo and behold, before two Appeal Court judges and with barely a whimper, Sugar's leave was granted!

In March 1994 I was forced to bring a negligence claim against my former solicitor and friend Bryan Fugler. Shortly following the purchase of my shares in Tottenham in June 1991, Bryan had also become an adviser to the club. I thought he was someone in whom both personally and professionally I could have complete trust. However, following my dispute with Sugar and my departure from Tottenham, Bryan chose to remain with Spurs and Sugar, and he told me he could no longer act for me on account of the conflict of interest.

I consequently transferred the responsibility for my legal affairs to Nick Trainer. Over the next six months I became progressively more convinced that problems of neglect and serious error were arising in matters over which Bryan had had charge: I therefore decided I had no alternative other than to bring the action.

Then in September 1994 I published my autobiography. This was the first opportunity for me to set out my time at Tottenham and my experiences with Alan Sugar. Almost as night follows day, Sugar and Tony Berry both sued for libel. This time I was not alone and had two co-defendants. They were the publishers of the book, Michael Joseph, and the newspaper that had published the serial, the *Mail on Sunday*.

Tony Berry's action came up for trial on 2 October 1995, which coincidentally, was just a week before England's away match against Norway! I can do no better than quote here my press statement at the time:

> Considering all the circumstances, today's settlement is a realistic compromise for all the defendants. I am also delighted that the settlement makes no provision for me to pay damages. There remains no doubt that documents relating to my business interests had been stolen from my offices and circulated widely to sections of the media in an attempt to discredit me.
>
> It appears, however, that certain evidence provided to us has proved unreliable. In the circumstances I am content that this action has been concluded and happy that Mr Berry has fully accepted that I acted with honesty and in good faith.

A few obvious journalists published reports I considered to be wildly inaccurate, but Tony Berry can hardly have been a happy man. He settled at the door to the court on terms which would not have covered his costs.

Alan Sugar's action continues unabated and might be described as having more tactical twists than a World Cup Final, some of which warrant a yellow card. That case is likely to be heard in the autumn of 1996.

Coincidentally, less than one month after having commenced proceedings against Bryan Fugler, his brother Jeff Fugler began insolvency proceedings against Scribes West. He alleged that some eighteen months earlier he had undertaken marketing services for which he had not been paid, and claimed almost £20,000. We have defended this action rigorously, convinced that such services were not provided even though requested and that the action was designed simply to bring pressure on me financially and to give the media another opportunity to attack my reputation.

More than any of the other actions I have faced, this has been the most distressful. We successfully defeated the insolvency proceedings in the summer of 1994, with the court ruling that the matter should go to a full trial.

There are very clear and precise guidelines set down by the court regarding the disclosure of evidence and of it being relative to the case in question. However, on 29 September 1995, with the action itself some eighteen months old, we were delivered another shock.

At 7.15pm the witness statement of Jeff Fugler was delivered by hand to Nick Trainer's officer (unsigned and out of time). It contained paragraphs which I decided would have been more at home in a James Bond movie. Jeff Fugler stated that he had been in Eddie's office at Tottenham on the day of the transfer of Teddy Sheringham in August 1992 – a fact which Eddie vehemently denies and on which other witnesses support him. Furthermore, he produced a series of copy invoices, never before seen by us, and a set of which I had no doubt I could prove were forgeries. His objective seems to be to reflect Alan Sugar's 'Clough likes a bung' allegation and discredit us before the court.

As if this was not enough, these documents appeared in the first edition of the *Daily Telegraph* in an article by Mihir Bose that very same day – we did not actually get to view copies of the documents until later the following week. On my instructions Eddie went to the Chelsea police and to the Premier League inquiry on the following Monday.

More shocks were to come. Shortly before the trial commenced, I came to believe that Herbert Smith (Alan Sugar's
solicitors) were actively supporting Fugler's action against me. In a
reply to Herbert Smith in a letter dated 23 November, 1995, Jeff
Fugler's solicitors, Karim, stated: 'You will recollect that your Mr
Watts on 3 November, 1995, under cover of a "compliment slip",
provided us with . . .'.

The origin of this document was Colin Sandy who is an associate of Sugar from Amstrad and a Tottenham director and one of
the documents quoted carried his fax number. Was this not further
evidence of a campaign to discredit me?

The trial actually took place in two halves, beginning in
November 1995, the same time as the England international
against Switzerland. It had originally been scheduled for three
days, but at the end of this time we had barely finished hearing
Fugler's argument, and the event had become a media circus,
which succeeded in wrapping the whole case in a blanket of
extreme prejudice. The judge was unable to sit longer than three
days and so the case was adjourned until mid-December. This gave
a further opportunity for the hostile elements of the media to run
riot. It duly resumed on Tuesday, 11 December, one day before
the game against Portugal.

My solicitor issued subpoenas for Mihir Bose and Harry Harris
to appear in court for cross-examination as to their roles in relation
to this matter. Both resisted our applications, but at the hearing
the acting judge (Recorder Williams) said to our counsel (David
Farrer QC), 'Do you want to convince me 105 per cent, when I
am already convinced 95 per cent?' Bose and Harris were not
ordered to give evidence at the trial and our counsel deduced from
the judge's remarks that he had completely accepted our points on
contempt and prejudice and did not therefore address these issues
any further in the second part of the trial. Regrettably, the final
judgement did not reflect the judge's implied attitude up to this
point, and in fact was contradictory to it.

Although we won a substantial reduction in Fugler's claim and
only paid part of the costs, the judge did little or nothing in dealing with the points of prejudice raised by my counsel. Speaking of
the *Daily Telegraph* and their publication of the forged invoices
and citing of Fugler's ulterior motives, the judge said, 'I am
fortified by the close proximity – one might say the *very* close

proximity – of the date that Mr Fugler's written statement was made available to the defendants and the date of publication of the invoices in the *Daily Telegraph*. I found the proximity of these events to be more than coincidental.'

When one considers that Bose wrote Irving Scholar's book, was the first journalist to write, in August 1993, of the documents stolen from my office, and maintains close relations with Alan Sugar's camp, that coincidence takes on a much more onerous perspective. When also seen in the light of my earlier comment on the contribution by Alan Sugar's solicitors Herbert Smith it seems rather more than coincidental. Yet the judge stated, 'I am not satisfied that they [the documents] were fed to the plaintiffs by a third party. I reject the conspiracy allegation that has been put forward at a late stage of the hearing.'

Dealing with the forged invoices the judge offered two explanations: '[they] could have been prepared as an April Fool's Day type joke . . . Another possibility is a rather more sinister one: that [they were] concocted in order to stir things, for one or other of the parties, presumably for the defendants.' Nevertheless, he again failed to find against Fugler and stated: 'I am led to a finding that Mr Fugler had an ulterior or improper motive . . . namely to bring pressure on the defendants . . . There is no evidence before me that Mr Fugler ever said to Mr Venables, or any one else at the defendant company, about being paid, otherwise he would blow the gaff or blow the whistle . . . It was more probably rather more subtle than that.' I was shocked by the awful realization that 'subtle' blackmail did not constitute a crime.

One senior professional attached to the case stated that 'Irreparable damage has been done to Mr Venables. If the Recorder did not, on fuller reflection, intend the full apparent implications of his extempore judgement, a considerable injustice has been done. In any case, nobody should see his reputation undone by such a seemingly ill-prepared and incoherent judgement. Surely such a case should never be handled by other than a most senior and experienced member of the judiciary. [These] criticisms cannot be aired in the Court of Appeal since they go only to a matter or credit . . .' In other words they were simply a matter of prejudice.

So much for natural justice! I was not impressed.

More blows were, however, destined. For more than a year,

senior police officers attached to Chelsea CID had been investigating complaints by me and Eddie and had registered a 'crime sheet' based upon conspiracy to pervert the course of justice. Between November and December 1995, during the trial proceedings, letters of complaint were written by Herbert Smith, Alan Sugar's solicitors, to an assistant commissioner for police concerning the officer in charge of the inquiry. These letters went as high as the Director of Public Prosecutions: meetings were convened.

Eddie and I then both received letters from a chief superintendant which stated: 'I have had the case reviewed by a senior detective not associated with this division. As a result of that review, supported by advice from the Metropolitan Police Solicitor's Department, I have come to the conclusion that it is not in the public interest for the police to continue with this investigation.'

Stifled once more!

In October 1993 I wrote to both the Football Association and the Premier League asking them to set up an inquiry. I had been the victim of some wild, false and malicious allegations and wanted my name cleared. I have shouldered the burden of this inquiry for almost two and a half years, throughout my term of employment with the FA, and regret to say that it has still not reported. The major allegations concerning the Paul Gascoigne transfer to Lazio and use of agents contrary to regulations have been dispelled by Gino Santin, demolishing the *Panorama* defence in his libel action.

The question of the 'Clough likes a bung' allegation persists and seems to have mesmerized the inquiry. I find the matter most frustrating. The Companies and Fraud Squad investigated this issue following a complaint by Alan Sugar, and after interviewing many witnesses over a period of some ten months, ceased the investigation. At the time of writing, this was more than eighteen months ago. I am particularly concerned about the delay in reporting as I know any finding by the Premier League will only go further in clearing my name. If this had happened twelve months ago I might have been telling a different story now.

After the *Panorama* programme in September 1993, and various complaints from predictable sources, my companies Scribes West Limited and Edennote faced investigations by the Department of Trade and Industry. In December 1995, following more than two years of enquiries, the DTI finally acted. However, for me this brought mixed blessings. I was delighted that my name was cleared of all criminal activity. Despite press speculation to the contrary, including deliberate leaks about my imminent arrest, the DTI have confirmed that they will not bring criminal proceedings against me.

Unfortunately though, the matter does not end there, as the DTI have brought proceedings against me in an attempt to disqualify me as a director. This is largely based on technical offences, and I will of course rigorously defend the case.

The vicious campaign against me by certain journalists over the last three years has resulted in my bringing a number of libel actions, the most noticeable of which are against *Panorama* and the *Daily Mirror*. I have also got several kept on ice, for action as soon as time and resources permit. It is impossible for any individual to mount a new libel action every week.

As well as the libel actions I have made a formal complaint to the Press Complaints Commission covering almost 140 articles from one newspaper journalist. Almost everyone I speak to tells me this is a waste of time, but we will persist and test the system. If natural justice is allowed to take its course, this will be the biggest case in the history of the PCC.

# CHAPTER EIGHTEEN

## TED AND THE JUNGLE OF MALAYA

Ted Buxton, my personal assistant and right-hand man at the FA, scouts round England and the world, reporting on our players and also the players who will be our opposition. I suppose scouting is not unlike doing a recce in the Army, and maybe that is why Ted is so good at it, as he has quite a colourful and varied past.

He was playing for Millwall when he was called up for National Service, and before he had time to think he was sent to fight in Malaya against the Chinese.

He had to rely on basic survival instincts and was caught in a four-day ambush. As soon as he arrived back from the ambush he was called in to see the commanding officer, who asked Ted to play for the British Army against Singapore. This was the crowning glory of his playing career: the British Army won 3–2 and Ted scored twice. Unfortunately, most of us missed his moment of glory as it took place in the Far East, but being in the war was a hell of an experience for him at such a young age. It was extremely character forming. Having to get along with a strange group of men who are all under extreme stress is not unlike fitting into a football team, and that is probably why Ted is so good at settling nervous players and helping to keep peace and harmony in the side. I'll let him tell his story:

'When I landed out in Malaya I hardly knew where it was let alone what I was going to be let in for. The conditions were incredible, really vile. I became a non-commissioned officer after only six weeks and was made corporal in charge of patrols.

Patrolling the jungle is nothing like zipping round London in a panda car. We also had to overcome all sorts of foul natural pests like Weil's disease.

'I was unfortunate to be caught in an ambush and from this I suffered a partially collapsed lung and a smashed right ear. I was treated by the medical guy, who in real life was an ex-baker with just six weeks' medical training! Not surprisingly he made a cock-up of things and forgot to take out a swab from my ear, with the result that I developed horrible flu-like symptoms and dizziness. It was ten days before they discovered the swab, which was some-what off by then.

'Just before Christmas 1953 we were dropped deep into the jungle to attack a Chinese camp. We used to be dropped in by heli-copter and I was always one of the first out as the old soldiers advised us the enemy often doesn't hit the first men out. This was supposed to be a four-day operation, but it turned into the biggest fight yet and became Operation Blick, which lasted four weeks rather than four days. When we hit the camp we discovered enemy information which later helped overcome the Chinese.

'In my first ambush I killed a couple of the enemy and wounded one. A couple of months after that I had a call from the CO, who told me I had to go and identify the wounded soldier as he was going to be hanged. I soon learnt the lesson that you don't bring back wounded enemy soldiers, you kill them as they have a fate worse than death waiting for them at the hands of their own people.

'I learnt a bit about the so-called weaker sex as one of our chief targets was a woman called Ahling. She had a husband who had been educated in England and when war had broken out he had killed Sir Henry Gurney the High Commissioner, so we had repaid the compliment by killing him. Then his wife took over. A couple of her kind at a football match would soon sort out trouble on the terraces. She was utterly vicious. When she and her troops cap-tured enemy soldiers they used to cut their testicles off and then skin them alive. However, we received good intelligence that she was going to be in a certain place at seven in the morning to pick up food.

'We staked out the place and sat up all night to wait. Finally, she walked into the clearing at eight in the morning, wearing a black pirate-type scarf. She picked up the things that were waiting for her and then started to walk towards where I was hidden in the jungle. I waited for the soldier in charge of us to give the signal to shoot, but nothing happened. She kept walking towards me and there was nothing I could do. In the end she escaped because the man in charge of us had fallen asleep! Not a moment of glory for the British Army.

'Shortly after that I served my time and returned through the alligator and crocodile-infested swamps to civilisation. The Millwall fans seemed like pussycats compared to that lot, and I have to say it was a long while before I stopped having nightmares about the whole experience. But I did learn some valuable lessons about living in a group where your life depended on the courage and quick thinking of your comrades. I've always felt at home in a team situation and I am immensely proud to be a part of the England set-up. Working with Terry for the Football Association is a dream come true. Terry is one of those rare blokes who believes in loyalty and integrity. When I lost my job at Tottenham after Terry lost his, he rang me every day just to keep my spirits up, in spite of the fact that he was facing daily ambushes by the tabloid journalists. I can think of a few who could do with the Ahling treatment!'

There aren't a lot of guys who are as loyal as Ted. He's also an excellent scout and has the ability to sum up a player accurately and concisely, which is exactly what I need. I have great admiration for him. Fighting for your country and facing up to the prospect of killing people is not something that we can face lightly.

After his antics in the jungle, Ted went to Chelsea as a non-contract player before starting coaching at Aldershot. His talents in the coaching sphere came to light when he went to Epsom & Ewell as a coach. The team were in the Surrey Senior League and they won numerous honours when Ted was with them. They ended up going to Wembley to play in the first ever FA Vase, which they lost 2–1 to Hoddesdon.

He then returned to Millwall as coach of the reserves and youth team. This was when I first got to know Ted, as Millwall won promotion by beating Crystal Palace, where I was then manager. During the 1975/76 season they went unbeaten for sixteen games. At that time Millwall fans had a very bad reputation, but they were just getting it right when *Panorama* (who else!) broadcast a programme which undid all the good and caused a lot more trouble.

Ted soon left our shores again to spend three years in the USA with Tampa Bay Rowdies at the time Rodney Marsh was there. He then returned and took over Gillingham with Keith Peacock. It was here that he pulled off the transfer deal of the century by getting Tony Cascarino in exchange for twelve tracksuits. Cascarino was playing for Crockenhill in Kent and they obviously needed a bit of kit. He eventually sold Cascarino to Millwall for £250,000. Now, of course, the player is in France with Marseille.

In 1985 Ted had a call from Peter Shreeves of Tottenham. At first Ted thought he was after Cascarino, but in fact Shreeves was after Ted, and asked him to take over from Bill Nicholson as chief scout. And that is how he came to work with me.

Ted and I hit it off immediately. We see things the same way, have the same sense of humour and like the same players. I was more than willing to give Ted all the responsibility he wanted. He was the man who went to watch Gazza play in Newcastle reserves and said he was a player for the future. He also recommended Richard Gough and Erik Thorstvedt. It's difficult to say what makes a great scout, but Ted is definitely one of the best. In describing how he spots a potential star he says: 'Like a lot of things, it's down to a gut feeling, you look at the balance and pace of the player, but really it's just something you feel.'

On his travels all over the world looking at players, Ted has even witnessed an execution. 'I was in Saudi Arabia trying to find a particular player, when I was awoken by a commotion outside my hotel window. I thought it was just the general chaos of a market, or something, but when I looked out of my window there was a guy being beheaded for adultery. The woman had already lost her head. It wasn't exactly what you expect to see in the square outside your hotel. But travelling as I do, I get to see some pretty strange sights. It's a good job we don't have that custom here or half our Government ministers would be headless!'

I was very pleased that I could pay back Ted's loyalty when I joined the FA. When I saw the state of the available information about our current opposition, I immediately sent for Ted. His title is Assistant to National Coach – Scouting, but in reality he is the chief scout, a new FA position. He has taken to the job like a duck to water. Thanks to Ted we now have a year's dossier on every player who is eligible to play for England, and extensive information on all our opponents.

Ted tells me that this new appointment has made his family and friends very proud; even his ex-wife rings up to get signed photos. I like seeing Ted's sons at Wembley, as it's my opinion that a family atmosphere is the best thing you can create around football matches, and we seem to be doing just that with our own environment around the England team.

Like me, Ted feels that, internationally, there is an ever-diminishing gap between the top teams and those who are supposed to be emerging. Look at the talent of the African nations during the last couple of World Cups, and look at Japan. A lot of people slaughtered us after the Japanese match in the Umbro summer tournament, but as Ted says: 'The Japanese played very well, and it is silly to put our team down; it's like Hungary again. Teams like Japan are becoming much more well organized and difficult to beat.'

# CHAPTER NINETEEN

## THE MEDIA MAN AND THE COMMERCIAL MAN

The number of journalists who follow the England team has doubled since the 1990 World Cup, and their demands and the way some of them sensationalize or invent things that simply do not exist is becoming more of a problem. It is almost impossible to bring some order into the mêlée of journalists, photographers and others, but the man charged with this awesome task is David Davies, who is the FA's Director of Public Affairs.

I like David's realistic and practical approach; he's very easy to talk to and, of course, knows his job very well. He was a journalist himself for twenty-two years, twenty-one of which were spent at the BBC. He was their political correspondent for six years and the education correspondent for four. He also presented *Songs of Praise, Come Dancing*, quiz shows and *Match of the Day*.

As we need to have good relations with the Government, David's experience in the political ring is vital in the lead up to the European Championship finals. David's main role is to ensure that the FA's points of view are effectively transported into the public domain. Previously, the FA had given no priority to explaining what it did, and why.

It is extremely difficult for a public body to be popular. Public bodies are often concerned with order and discipline and are seen as the headmasters of the people they represent. But it is crucial to be reactive and proactive. David says, 'I want people to be aware of what we are doing, and why we are doing it.' David has set up his own department over the last year and an indication of just how successful he's been was amply demonstrated when an editorial in *The Times* on Cup Final day praised the FA and his department.

David also says it has helped him to have me as England Coach as I know the workings of the media quite well. After the shenanigans of the last couple of years it would be odd if I didn't! But I do watch television, listen to the radio and read the newspapers, and generally take an interest. However, as David says, we are not going to be a punchbag or take any chicanery from the media. We are dedicated to winning at least one, if not two, major football tournaments within the next four years. Carlos Alberto Parreira stressed the importance of knowing that everything was in place off the pitch. Well, David is my captain off the pitch; he ensures that we have a smooth path and cool efficiency all along the way, so I can concentrate on football and getting the team together.

David says, 'I am no more or less than a football fan who has been lucky enough to find himself working at the highest level of the game. I want to do my bit to ensure that everything works well. This is the only job I would have left the BBC for. But a chance like this comes up once in a lifetime, and you just can't turn it down. There have been a few surprises; I have been overwhelmed by the sheer intensity of interest. At the end of the day you are never finished, and I have been seriously impressed by some of the people at the FA.'

We were both of the same opinion regarding the summer tournament. We felt it went down very well and we both learnt lessons. I was happy with the introduction of the 'mixed zone', which means having more informal Press gatherings in the dressing room and other areas, rather than formal press conferences; but we still need to do a lot of work to make it perfect.

I was surprised to learn from David that 310,000 tickets had been sold for matches in June 1996 and the people who bought them before December 1995 didn't even know which teams they would be seeing. Eleven and a half to twelve million pounds had already been taken, which shows just how much enthusiasm there is for the European Championship finals.

It cannot be stressed how important Government relations are. David goes to Westminster about once a week to talk to the departments who will be involved in the tournament. He has close contact with the Home Secretary regarding security. His worst memory from the time he has been in the job is the same as mine:

the riots in Dublin. Whereas I was shut away down in the dressing-room not really knowing exactly what was going on, David was in the thick of it. He was sitting just along from Ted Buxton in the stand.

Like all of us, he just didn't expect any trouble: 'For a minute I just couldn't believe what was going on, and then I just got on with doing what I had to do. My first port of call was to get the relevant people together, like Graham Kelly and you, and ensure the security people were all gathered in one place so the media could get access to you all. Once we'd realized the game wasn't going on, then we had to deal with it. I was determined that the FA would get across its disgust with the situation. It's not enough to say that most football fans are decent, law-abiding people who go along to support their team; we must all actively seek to isolate the troublemakers. We are doing everything within our power to make sure that going to a football match is a safe, enjoyable experience. Apart from this we want to be European Champions.'

The FA has often been accused of being full of fuddy-duddies, but it is becoming more and more removed from this accusation. I don't feel I belong to this category, and there are many members of the FA who certainly do not fit this description; such as Pat Smith, who is the first woman deputy chief executive. Recently the FA Council took a decision that the Executive Committee of the FA should have executive powers. This may be obvious, but it hadn't been like that. The objective is that decisions should be taken more quickly, and there should be a sharper, more focused response to events.

David called a press conference at 7.30am on the morning after the Dublin riots and followed this up with another conference at 4.30pm, so you can't accuse us of being fuddy-duddy over that. We are getting geared up for the twenty-first century. When you think about it the FA has a huge responsibility in being involved in football, all the way from the grass roots to the World Cup.

David and I think that the FA has more than proved it can handle unforeseen problems, such as the Cantona incident and the George Graham investigation. Someone has to see the wider aspect and the implications of complex issues outside of their local club; and this is the job of the FA. And I for one am glad to be part of it. We just have to keep our heads and ensure that problems that arise are put into perspective; there's no point in over-reacting.

One of the most helpful things to come out of this increase in input such as in the fixtures list and more power in making decisions is that I will have more time with the team in the build-up to the European Championship finals.

## The Commercial Man

Trevor Philips, the FA's Commercial and Marketing Director is in charge of the FA's commercial interests. He came to the FA from the Football League, where he was headhunted from Beecham.

Trevor now freely admits that his arrival in the football world was a baptism of fire. In normal commercial business you follow the rules and regulations of common business practice. If a project makes good commercial sense with both parties benefiting from the association, then generally you go ahead and agree it. However, football is not like that, or rather wasn't like that – it was full of people who were suspicious of commercial ventures. So Trevor has had an uphill struggle to implement a sound commercial policy that will lead us into the twenty-first century.

For example, when he arrived at the FA he found that Wembley had a contract which was to run until 2002, which effectively gave it control of all the prime commercial possibilities, such as perimeter boards. In practice this meant that the FA had no commercial control over the environment in which England played their matches, and Trevor had nothing to negotiate with. You could bring in Coca-Cola as a main sponsor and then arrive on match day to find that Pepsi-Cola had bought the perimeter boards.

There followed a long, bitter battle which Trevor won after a high-profile press campaign in which the FA threatened to move the Cup Final away from Wembley to Twickenham. This resulted in the Wembley share price falling and so the Wembley directors were forced to the negotiating table. A new contract was signed which pooled all rights into a joint venture called Total Football. This now generates about £6,000,000 a year.

The other problem that Trevor has is that interest in the England team is linked to its success. After the disastrous 1988 and 1992 European Championship finals, interest fell, but after the successful 1990 World Cup interest was high again.

There are two essential commodities: the FA Cup and the England International Senior team. However, the function of the

FA is not just about making money. The FA Cup also has enormous historical value and so it is not possible to over-commercialize it by selling the rights to satellite TV, or losing the title to a sponsor. It must always be the FA Cup sponsored by x, y or z.

In 1992 the total income generated from domestic television, overseas television, sponsorship and licensing was £13.7 million. This year it will be £40.1 million and in the year 2000 £62.6 million; so there has been tremendous progress made under Trevor, who has also succeeded in keeping a delicate balance between over-commercialization and maintaining the historical value of the FA products.

Euro 96 may not generate a huge amount of income but Trevor and I both see the event as a long-term investment for the future of English football. If people leave England having had a really good time and have been impressed by the tournament organization then the sponsors will leave some of their dollars here to the future benefit of English football. Trevor is proving the FA can provide commercial success whilst still retaining its essential mystique.

# Chapter Twenty

## Holidays, High Days and Countdown Towards the European Championship Finals

As the new season was approaching, I began to think about how things could be generally improved in soccer. The fans want to see good, entertaining games, and we need to reward attacking teams for their performance. The big question is, how can we do this?

I think the answer is to alter the present points system. I do think that we have moved a step forward by giving three points for a victory, so that both teams have a stronger incentive to win. But I don't think we have gone far enough.

I would like to see four points for a win, two points for a score draw, and no points for a goalless draw. You can argue that you can have some good 0–0 matches, but I would say that you have failed to capture the spirit of the game, which is to score goals and to keep it attractive. That's why football is the best game in the world. I don't think we should rest on our laurels. Nowadays kids find other interests, like watching *Gladiators*, and if we aren't careful soccer could lose out. We could find that the kids who knock a ball around the street will be playing rugby or cricket.

We have to make progress. Initially, I would like to experiment more with the lower leagues to see how things work. If the revised points system does work, it can be brought into the game on a permanent basis. If it doesn't, then at least we are trying.

**Jürgen Klinsmann**
On the 27 August, the *Mail on Sunday* published an article which echoed a conversation I had with Jürgen Klinsmann.

The headline blasted: 'KLINSMANN: I WANTED TO STAY.' The journalist, Simon Greenberg, had gone down to Germany to interview Jürgen and discover exactly why he left the club. Jürgen said he had asked Alan Sugar what his plans were for the new season and how much money he was going to invest in new players. The answer was very little, and so Jürgen had decided that it would be better to move.

## My trips abroad

During the summer recess, which these days seems less of a recess than a slight pause before the next season gets underway, I took a few trips abroad to see what other countries were doing with the beautiful game.

One of my first stops was South Africa. It was a pleasure to return to such a beautiful country. Now that the political system has changed, I hope that it will once again become a sporting power. South Africa won the Rugby World Cup, and there is certainly no shortage of enthusiasm for sport. Now South Africa has also won the Africa Nations Cup.

Several top international sportsmen have already been to the country to see how they can help in the development of a strong sporting structure, and recently England Under-17s beat South African Under-17s 2–0. They asked me to go along and coach in the townships and take a look at the young players. The whole trip was about improving relations with South Africa.

I bumped into Charlie Hughes (the FA's coaching adviser) on the flight. And it transpired he was going out to help the South African Football Association himself.

We had a lot of television coverage both in South Africa and throughout Europe on Sky of me coaching in Boksburg and Mamelodi. I also did quite a few interviews on local radio and television to spread the gospel about what football can do for the country and also what I thought about the youngsters and how they are developing.

I found a lot of talent down there, but I did notice that the young players seemed to be physically frail and looked younger than their age. This is probably due to the maize diet and they need to look at their diet and change it to something more substantial if they want to produce players who are physically stronger. However, I expect this will have to wait until the economy is more

*Clockwise from top left:* Dennis Wise, Paul Gascoigne, Jamie Redknapp and John Scales (© *Popperfoto*)

*Clockwise from top left:* Nick Barmby, Gary Pallister, Graeme Le Saux and Alan Shearer (© *Popperfoto*)

*Clockwise from top left:* Tony Adams, Teddy Sheringham, David Platt and Steve McManaman (© *Popperfoto*)

*Above* Darren Anderton, *below* Warren Barton (© *Popperfoto*)

John Barnes (© *Popperfoto*)

Terry and Scottish coach Craig Brown, in Birmingham on 17 December 1995 after the European Championship Draw put England and Scotland together in Group A (© *Popperfoto*)

Terry's daughters Nancy (*left*) and Tracey (*right*)

Terry's grandson Sammy at Madame
Tussaud's in February 1996

Terry, Yvette and Pelé

Sophie, the beloved running partner of the late, great Bobby Moore, in
celebration of life and love

stable. I think if they could combine physical strength with their talent they would become a very strong footballing nation. I found plenty of enthusiasm and motivation amongst the kids, and they were very keen to talk about how they could improve and develop their skills. It is always a joy to work with youngsters who really want to learn and will put themselves out, both for themselves and the good of the team.

When I assess players I look at four main characteristics: technical, tactical, personality and pace. A player with 10 out of 10 for all four, a total of 40 points, is world class. There aren't any English players that have scored that magic number, but I hope we won't be too far off reaching that soon. It is important that a player will think of the team and work hard for the others.

I do believe that if you get players when they are young you can have an influence on their personality. When Glenn Hoddle was in the Under-21s, I asked him how he had learnt to master the ball so well. He replied that it was through watching Brazil play on television as a child; so outside factors can affect kids greatly. If Glenn hadn't watched Brazil and it hadn't sparked off an interest, then we wouldn't have enjoyed his talent. At the moment I think that the way we build talent is too haphazard. We need to develop a proper system. It is more by chance than anything else that we have highly skilled players like Gazza and Redknapp.

The coach has a huge amount of responsibility in influencing a child. Seven is the ideal age to start, but if the coach isn't good enough, and the kid picks up bad habits, then it will be difficult to change them at a later stage.

I believe that all of us in the game need to get together to discuss the future and talk about how we can improve our talent and move into a new era. I consider going abroad and meeting and coaching other nations to be a vital part of my job. South Africa is emerging. In ten years time they may be potential World Champions and then I will have had some insight into how it all began and how they have evolved.

A good example of a more dynamic approach was that taken by the Dutch, who came over to observe Liverpool in the 1980s. They thought they had worked out the formula for success, but they didn't rest on their laurels – instead they added more to it and produced outstanding teams like Ajax.

I believe the pace of the game has to be dictated from the back, and when it's not possible to get the ball forward quickly we have to keep it until we find our players strategically placed to go forward. Ajax have perfected the system with three at the back and, though they might play slowly in the last two-thirds of the field, in the final third they have extreme pace on the flanks, which is hard to cover: if you're committed there, you leave gaps in the middle.

South Africa may have a way to go before they produce an outstanding team such as Ajax, but in my mind they are on the right path not only because they have talent, but because they are willing to adopt that most elusive of things – an open mind. I hope that in England we are also willing to look at our tactics and adapt to meet the challenges of the future.

The England team were once World Champions. We are now 22nd in the FIFA world rankings. If we want to improve, it is up to everyone involved in the game, not just me as England Coach. Change must come from the coaches who teach the youngsters of nine or ten, as well Premier League managers. I can only work with what I am given, and the better that is the more chance we have of regaining past glory.

I hope we play against South Africa in the next couple of years. I intend to keep in touch with the South Africans and will be interested to see how the players and the team develop.

## Postcard from the Seychelles

After South Africa my wife and I managed to get a few days holiday in the Seychelles, one of the most naturally beautiful islands I have seen. The swimming opportunities are second to none. Unfortunately, we have slightly different views of what we like doing on holiday. She has to put up with a bag full of football videos, and is always embarrassed when we check-in to the hotel and I ask for a video recorder to be sent to the room. She feels that the hotel staff probably think we are a couple of perverts with a bag full of x-rated porn videos! As I ask for the video she is always quick to say, 'It's only football videos.'

## South Carolina

Whereas South Africa was very much a hands-on approach, where I was involved in running around a football pitch, my trip to South Carolina was about talking about football rather than playing it.

Umbro, the sportswear company who provide the official strip and other related clothing to the England team, invited me to become a member of their 'star chamber'. This is a concept that they have created to discuss how the game of football may evolve to meet the demands of the twenty-first century.

I was very pleased to be involved, especially as they have only invited a restricted few to participate in this think tank.

Louis van Gaal, the manager of Ajax, was there, and so was the great Pelé and the Japanese National Coach Shu Kamo. Peter Gooding from the American Football Federation was also present. I was amazed to learn from him that they have 12,000 coaches as members throughout America. This is absolutely incredible as I don't think we have 1,200 in Britain. I know that America is a lot bigger, but we are supposed to have a long tradition as a footballing nation, whereas our type of football, or soccer as it is known over there, has never been one of the most popular sports in America. It makes you wonder what will happen if soccer really does take off in the United States.

At the South Carolina meeting one vital question dominated the discussion: Where is football going to be in ten years time?

Football is the most popular sport in the world. Can we afford to just sit back and allow it to blossom and develop by itself? Of course the answer to that was a big NO. We have to make sure it is still the most popular game in ten years time.

Over the course of three days, we talked about the present state of football and how we may change things. Several interesting points came out of the sessions. We all had similar basic concerns about the wellbeing of the game we love. These included: the consequences of commercial influence, including television rights, fees, sponsors, transfer market changes with money going to players; the integrity of the game, particularly professional influences on youth development; reconciling huge expenditures to promote the game while many clubs remain in the red; football becoming just another entertainment vehicle; the divergent interests of coaches (on the field, long-term) and directors' and chairmens' commercial interests (off the field, short-term return); player-development too often being only performance-based rather than looking at the complete character; and football as a brand not representing itself well enough.

We concluded that the increasing wealth of the game must be aligned with an improvement in quality. There appears to be an essential conflict between the owners and administrators of the clubs, who emphasize wealth at the expense of quality, and coaches and players who think that if the game gets 'better' then riches will follow.

Regarding the commercial conflicts, we came to the conclusion that television is not necessarily an enemy. While TV companies' objectives are aggressive (e.g. power, viewers, financial return, eliminating competitors), they do fund football and often think long-term. The key to improving relations is for television owners and football to have similar objectives, and develop football in a positive way for the future. Over-commercialization is evident when television dictates unsatisfactory playing arrangements. It is dangerous to think only of the money that television can offer. If you go with the highest bidder, you can lose control. What happens if you get £X million one year and write that into your budget, only to have the television station reduce the amount or even drop it altogether in a year or two? When television pays megabucks for exclusive rights to a sport, it is thinking only commercially. If the viewing figures drop, you are out and they are on to another sport. You can't sell your soul without risking high stakes.

After the first day we also came to the conclusion that too many teams play with the aim of not losing rather than winning. We need a new creative attitude in football. We also need to ensure that professional coaches hold some sort of qualification. A lot of the managers of professional clubs hold no formal coaching qualifications. This is unacceptable.

On day two we set about looking at the power structure and how to make the game more attractive. We have to recognize that football is in the entertainment business as well as being a sport. We have to look at the rules and decide if changes are necessary; it was considered that the FIFA Rules Task Force had been too conservative. In three years, there have been five meetings, only three recommendations for rule changes, and one actual change (the back-pass rule).

At the moment the marketing of football is left up to the sponsors, which means sponsors can dictate football's image. Football needs a global image based on the concept of the 'team'. We also have to promote football from the grass roots level, otherwise all we will be doing is papering over the cracks and ignoring the need for long-term change. As I've mentioned, the important thing is to concentrate on kids of six and seven who are just getting into football. We need to stimulate and sustain their interest in the game.

The magic of football is the link between the team and the fans. The key to all our decisions is to improve this relationship. Team owners and directors are in a position to strength this relationship. However, there are many external and internal factors which influence the decision makers. These vary from journalists, coaches and players, to the fans themselves. Somewhere along the line we have to make sure that football is governed by the right kind of leadership. Leaders who really care about the game are vital. They have to have integrity and want to put more quality and excitement into the game than they expect to earn, in monetary terms, out of it.

When we got down to discussing rule changes, we had some interesting and maybe innovatory suggestions. I have already mentioned it but I do think we should remove the timekeeping responsibilities from the referee and use a visible, public time clock, like they do in basketball. We should not allow television to influence playing conditions, such as narrowing the pitch or shortening the warm-up time. We also decided that my suggestion of a different points system, as already explained in a previous chapter, would be a good idea. And we also thought that only players who were behind the ball in defensive positions when a foul occurred could form a wall.

I thoroughly enjoyed the chance to get together with some of the best football brains in the world and thrash out a vision for the future. In three days, though, we just scratched the surface.

# Chapter Twenty-One

## Ajax – The Way Forward

Since the mid-1960s, Ajax have been one of the major forces in European and world club football. This is not down to the fact that they pour endless amounts of money into the club; in fact Ajax do not have substantial wealth to support them. Their success has been built on the efficient creation of more footballers.

Ajax have a strong youth policy to create their own home-grown talent, and they use this to build wealth. Recently, they had a change of view regarding the person who would be appointed head of the youth section. In the past the head of the youth section had been promoted to first team coach, but when Louis Van Gaal moved up to be replaced by Co Adriaanse, Ajax decided that the position of director of youth was important enough to stand on its own merit. Therefore Adriaanse who developed their present structure whereby they look after boys from eight to eighteen years of age has been offered a contract until he is sixty-five, and has made it clear that he does not wish to be coach of the first team. Ajax is run by a five-man board of elected directors and Adriaanse reports to one of these directors rather than Louis Van Gaal.

| Team Name | Age | No. in group | No. of sessions | No of matches | Opposition |
|-----------|-----|--------------|-----------------|---------------|------------|
| A1 | U18 | 16 | 6X | 26 | Same Age |
| A2 | U17 | 16 | 5X | 22 | One year older |
| B1 | U16 | 16 | 4X | 22 | Same Age |
| B2 | U15 | 16 | 4X | 22 | One year older |
| C1 | U14 | 16 | 3X | 22 | Two years older |
| C2 | U13 | 16 | 3X | 22 | One year older |
| D1 | U12 | 16 | 3X | 22 | Two years older |
| D2 | U11 | 16 | 3X | 22 | One year older |
| E1 | U10 | 16 | 3X | 22 | One year older |
| E2 | U9 | 16 | 3X | 22 | Two years older |

The number of games shown above is supplemented by friend-lies and tournament football to a maximum of a further fifteen games. Each team is assigned a voluntary team leader, who is always an ex-Ajax player, to reinforce the Ajax way of playing football.

Below E2 is the F group of 6–8 year olds and in order to orga-nize the best 16 intake at U8 they organize large trialling and training sessions. They have three 'Ajax' days when, at three sepa-rate amateur clubs in and around Amsterdam, kids at the F and E age are invited to play in four-a-side games, individual skill games, watch videos and meet the first team.

From these events the best kids are invited to the regular 'talent' days at Ajax's training ground. Assessment is discussed amongst all the youth staff and the chief scout, Tom Pronk. Eventually the best sixteen are chosen.

The attitude of the coaches is that winning is important, but it's not everything. I believe that kids should learn to enjoy kicking a ball around before they feel they have to win at all costs. Before Christmas each team's coach is encouraged to give games to all the boys, but after Christmas he is allowed to pick his strongest team.

Every week the coach of each team has an individual meeting with Adriaanse to discuss performances and any problems the boys may be having. Adriaanse also uses these sessions to assess the performance of the coach himself; a high standard is continually maintained.

The boys take fifteen physical and skill tests three times throughout the season. These tests have been evolved to measure mainly physical progress.

Ajax are always keen to involve the parents of the boys, and at Christmas each boy and his parents have a meeting with Adriaanse, his own coach and the team leader. A document, not unlike a school report, is discussed; it is very detailed, giving the pupil marks on each aspect of his technique, play and personality. Each child is given an overall mark. A grade A means that he is doing very well, and if he continues at this level, he will be kept on for the next season; B indicates that he has done all right, but there is no guarantee of being kept on for the next season; C means that unless there is a dramatic improvement there is little chance of him being kept on.

The pressure of these assessments is maintained until April, when a final evaluation is made. If a boy is told that he is not going to be kept on he has until 31 May to trial and be taken on by another club. Despite all this pressure only about two or three boys leave each year to be replaced by others, highlighting that the original assessment is very accurate and avoids causing unnecessary heartache to boys who pin all their hopes on becoming full-time Ajax players.

Tom Pronk is responsible for professional and schoolboy scouting. Ajax are allowed to sign boys within a 90-kilometre radius of Amsterdam. To cover this area there are part-time scouts who watch games at all levels.

The club has a footballing philosophy embodied in the phrase: T.I.P.S.:

T – Technique – number one requirement for an Ajax player
I – Intelligence – vital for their style of play
P – Personality – they have to be a team player
S – Speed, of thought and action

The scouts are told to look for these attributes in reverse order: S.P.I.T. Speed and personality are considered to be vital as they are God-given and can only be marginally improved. Ajax coaches feel they can improve the intelligence and technique of boys.

It is a wonderful opportunity for kids to be taken on by Ajax, but it is quite a heavy regime. Between the ages of eight and fourteen the boys train three or four times a week, they play on Saturday and, if the first team is playing at home on a Sunday, they are expected to attend the match with their team group. This means a total of five trips to and from the ground in a week. Some boys live an hour's drive from the stadium, so this is a major commitment for the parents to take on, especially if they have other children to look after, or are a one-parent family. Sometimes the clubs don't realize that they need to provide some kind of back-up for parents. Not only is a child's career in football time consuming but it is also financially draining.

As far as actual training is concerned, all the boys have football aerobics classes of thirty minutes each week for movement, balance and co-ordination. No matter how talented a kid is he has to learn to maintain good balance and be able to co-ordinate his movements quickly and efficiently. These classes could be the reason why European footballers have such skill in midfield; they don't just use power and force, as we tend to do, but they can turn on the ball with speed and maintain possession very well.

All groups have speed and athletic training to teach correct and efficient running techniques. This work is supported by visits to the well-equipped gymnasium, and advice from a part-time dietician who, as well as helping the boys, also gives advice to the parents regarding the best foods for their children to eat. The food produced at the club is prepared under her guidance. Diet is extremely important for growing lads who at different times in their lives will need more protein or carbohydrate to help build muscle and energy.

A physiotherapist has the complete medical history of all the boys from the age of eight, and the club also employs nine part-time teachers to help the boys with their homework in the afternoons. If a boy does badly at school then he has to miss training, which is a good incentive to keep up with the others in his group. If an Ajax youth team attends a tournament during term time then one of the teachers accompanies them to tutor all the boys while they are away.

From fourteen upwards, the club has implemented a new system of specialist training for their best players. This works on an individual basis and relates specifically to the positions individuals play.

In the Netherlands there are very strict rules governing the qualifications coaches require to be allowed to coach. We must implement a similar structure here. It simply isn't good enough for an ex-player to be able to get a top job in football just because he has played football. He needs not only his experience but formal teaching on how to convey certain information in an effective way to his team members. Just because you were good at maths at school doesn't mean you can walk into a class and teach maths. Likewise the best players have not always turned into the best managers. Sometimes if someone is brilliant at something, they find it difficult to explain their skill to others as it just comes naturally, and they cannot understand why everyone can't do it. You have to remember to keep things simple and as uncomplicated as possible.

*Coaching Qualifications in Holland*

| Qualification | Cost | Time |
| --- | --- | --- |
| Youth Soccer Licence | Negligible | A basic qualification takes 6 months to pass |
| Trainer – Coach III | Approx £400 | Start September. 20 theory sessions, 20 practical, 6 months. |
| Trainer – Coach II | Approx £800 | Start September, 20 theory, 20 practical, 6 months |

After this qualification you will not be accepted on the next course unless you have done 2–3 years practical work as Head Coach of an amateur Club or Assistant Coach at a pro-club.

The FA is currently creating a diploma in conjunction with UEFA. If you don't have that diploma, in a few years you will not be able to work in Europe, and you shouldn't be able to work in England. A taxi driver has to do two years of knowledge riding around London on a bike before he can be an official black cab driver, so why should it be any different for a football coach? Why shouldn't he have to do a course and pass exams before he can coach a team?

With all their preparation, it's a wonder we ever get to score a goal against the Dutch. This kind of organization is streets ahead of our 'suck it and see' type of attitude. We have some wonderful talent, but it needs nurturing, and there is no better way than to bring a player up through the ranks of a club to the senior squad. When I was at Tottenham I brought in young players like Nick Barmby and Darren Anderton with the objective of bringing them on to play in the senior side. In Anderton's case this has happened, but it was a shame that Tottenham felt they had to sell Nick Barmby.

As you will have gathered I am a great admirer of the Dutch. They not only have a very committed attitude towards the young players who are their future, but they also have great integrity in their dealings with each other. The media there seem to be most interesting. When I was at Barcelona, journalists from all over the world would come and interview me. I always found the Dutch press very educated football-wise. The clubs have a code of conduct that prohibits poaching of boys, and it appears that this is adhered to. However, if a boy is unhappy at the club he can leave by just filling out a transfer form before the annual 31 May deadline.

It is estimated that it costs Ajax about one million pounds a year to run their youth section. Considering the continuous quality of the players produced and the income derived from them when they are eventually sold, it is a very sound investment.

Ajax have played the same way for about thirty years. It is a loose 3-4-3 formation that has brought them a lot of glory. My prime objective in preparing my team for the European Championship finals is to have such flexibility.

# CHAPTER TWENTY-TWO

## EUROPEAN MANAGERS' MEETING
## AND COLOMBIA

For a long time I have believed that the England Coach could benefit from an exchange of views with Premier League managers.

However, it is rather difficult to get club managers round a table to express their views as they are loathe to give away secrets which could benefit their rivals. But I thought about this and decided there was an alternative option that would suit everyone. The one main thing that links us is that several Premier League clubs compete in the European cups, and England often play against European teams.

Bearing this in mind I approached Gordon Milne, chairman of the managers' union, and he very kindly agreed to arrange a meeting with most of the club managers involved in Europe: Alex Ferguson of Manchester United, Ray Harford of Blackburn Rovers, Roy Evans of Liverpool, Frank Clark of Nottingham Forest, and David Williams, who came along to represent Howard Wilkinson, as Howard had a prior commitment.

I cannot begin to say how valuable it was to meet up and exchange views. We had four hours together, but it seemed like ten minutes. We spent most of the time addressing tactical problems and trying to decide on the best system with which to beat European teams who basically play a different system to us.

The discussion revolved around:

1. What difference, if any, do the English teams expect in Europe as opposed to the Premier League?

2. Combating the more sophisticated tactical play from foreign teams.

3. The English game, being a gung-ho approach, is based on both sides attacking fast from the first moment of the game. But fast doesn't necessarily mean better, although it makes for better television entertainment.

4. Foreign teams not making mistakes at the back and making you chase the ball.

It was a session of pooling ideas. We all felt that a major problem is how to maximize ourselves in midfield. If English teams play with four at the back, and the opposition play with one or two strikers, we find that we've got our extra men at the back while they have theirs in midfield. And midfield is an area where the European teams are often technically superior to us, so even if we match their four in midfield we're still likely lose out. Furthermore, we're at a natural disadvantage as we tend only to play three in midfield.

To counteract this problem a deeper analysis of the systems the opposition may adopt is required. If the opposition plays a long-ball game, then we need more men at the back. However, if we are playing against a team that likes to play through the midfield, then more men are needed in midfield, and to do that you either have to take players from the front and bring them backwards, or take them from the back and bring them forwards, or both. This requires a system that can adapt itself fairly easily.

Our most difficult problem – scoring goals and preventing the opposition from scoring, may seem like stating the obvious, but how you resolve it tactically is not so simple.

Now that we are fully into the age of the computer we have statistics pouring out of our ears. Statisticians tell us that 50–60 per cent of goals come from set pieces (i.e. free-kicks and corner kicks). Therefore, we have to accept that we want set pieces, but we don't want to give them away. The players must have firmly stamped in their minds the fact that they shouldn't give away free-kicks round the box. This was a hard lesson we had to learn against Brazil.

We also discussed what is required from the front players once the ball is lost. Do you try and win it back in their first third of the pitch or do you try and win it in yours?

The statistics show that the majority of goals are scored by winning the ball back in the opposition's defensive third of the pitch.

Less goals are scored when the ball is picked up in midfield and even less from the back third. If you push players up and the ball is not past them, the opposition can slice through three or four of your players and get through to the last five. The kind of decisions you have to make are where do you want to try and win the ball back? What do you want your forwards to do? Do they go forward with the ball or drop back? Pressing means going up to the ball and trying to win it back. Where do you press? And when? Arrigo Sacchi, the Italian national team coach believes that 'a happy player is one in possession of the ball'. He teaches that pressing is very important and all midfielders and defenders should try to win the ball. At the same time the defence must be solid.

I believe you should try to win the ball back if the opposition doesn't have control, or you can arrive at your man at the same time as the ball. If the opposition passes well, let them come to you. Before the Colombia match I was still fine-tuning the team, but I do believe the correct path lies in trying to form a team that is easily flexible, can shift between a Christmas tree or diamond formation, and is capable of closing gaps wherever they appear.

### The Squad
David Seaman – Arsenal
Tim Flowers – Blackburn Rovers
Rob Jones – Liverpool
Gary Neville – Manchester United
Tony Adams – Arsenal
Steve Howey – Newcastle United
Gary Pallister – Manchester United (went home)
Graeme Le Saux – Blackburn Rovers
Stuart Pearce – Nottingham Forest
Steve McManaman – Liverpool
Robert Lee – Newcastle United
Jamie Redknapp – Liverpool
David Batty – Blackburn Rovers
Neil Ruddock – Liverpool
John Barnes – Liverpool
Paul Gascoigne – Rangers
Dennis Wise – Chelsea
Teddy Sheringham – Tottenham Hotspur
Peter Beardsley – Newcastle United (went home)

Nick Barmby – Middlesbrough
John Salako – Coventry City
Alan Shearer – Blackburn Rovers

An England international wouldn't be the same without the media blowing hot and hysterical over the inclusion or exclusion of one of the players.

This time it was Paul Ince. As soon as I announced the squad they were at it. Apparently I'd left him out because he wasn't committed; he was being snubbed because he had let me down for the summer tournament. The truth of the matter was that I felt Paul needed a settling-in period at his new club before he was subjected to more pressure. When a player goes to play abroad, particularly in a soccer-mad nation like Italy, he has to devote time to settling in and finding his feet. I spoke to Paul and we agreed to play things by ear. I said I'd come out and see him in a month or so and he seemed happy with that, but in fact he has had more problems settling in, so I think it would be better to leave him to concentrate on his club football for the time being. He also needs to bring his confidence back up.

I wanted to have a look at some of the younger players and give them an opportunity to see how they dealt with international football. I looked at four very young players. McManaman, Redknapp and Barmby, who had been in the Under-21s, and Gary Neville.

I'm keen to maintain a more fluid situation, whereby a player starts in the Under-21s and then progresses seamlessly into the senior squad.

ENGLAND V COLOMBIA 6 September 1995
Wembley stadium
Attendance: 20,038
England: Seaman, Neville, Le Saux, Redknapp (Lee 75), Adams, Howey, Barmby, Gascoigne (Barnes 75), Shearer (Sheringham 75), McManaman, Wise.
Colombia: Higuita, Santa, Mendoza, Bermudez, Perez, Alvarez, Lozano (Quiñones 46), Rincon, Valderrama, Asprilla, Valenciano
Result: 0–0
Referee: M Batta (France)

In fact, right from the word go, I brought four Under-21 players into the senior squad to make them feel comfortable: Fowler, Sol Campbell, Redknapp and Barmby.

We got good reviews after this match. Colombia are rated one of the best ball-keeping teams in the world, and are excellent passers. I wanted to see if we could go in and get the ball from them. Colombia are probably the best team at keeping the ball short in small areas, and possess a maestro in Carlos Valderrama.

However, I thought we more than held our own against them. In fact we hit the bar three times and we should have won the game. Their goalkeeper, Rene Higuita, made a save that must go down in history as the most spectacular of all time. It is a move he calls the 'scorpion kick' as he moves his body like a striking scorpion. It was just amazing to watch. None of us sitting on the bench could believe it. It looked as if the ball would go in the net when suddenly Higuita threw himself forwards in the air and kicked it out with both feet behind him. Unbelievable!

I introduced my third and most recent system in this match: a further development from system two, which I used for the USA game. I put in three forward players, who would go wide and also move into the box, I had one player in the hole behind the front players, and then two in midfield and four at the back. The idea was that one of the central defenders would move forward and make a third midfield player. This is a very mobile way of playing and immediately puts the opposition on the back foot, as they have to mark the forward players. It creates space for us to move into with the ball. It also creates a tight defensive system at the back.

I have now got two players for each position which satisfies one of my objectives.It gives the players an extra edge and keeps them on their toes. Newcastle have created a similar situation.

In this match Gazza played in midfield alongside Redknapp, so we had two good footballing players in the middle of the park, which I think at the top level is important: the more ball-passing players we have in midfield the more successful we can be. Both Gazza and Redknapp had a strong impact in midfield. Barmby also combined with Shearer very well. At half-time I tried to get Howey to go further forward, with and without the ball, to get in there quicker and help the midfield to outnumber the opposition. He did what he could, but he found it a little strange as he doesn't play like that with Newcastle.

# CHAPTER TWENTY-THREE

## AWAY TO NORWAY

What can I say about Norway that hasn't been said? The country has become the one we have to beat. And in recent times, it is not difficult to see why.

Norway do not play the most beautiful football, but they are difficult to beat because they are so defensive. They haven't lost at home for four years (nineteen games), and in that time they've only conceded seven goals. And, of course, they stopped us going to the World Cup two years ago.

**The Squad**
David Seaman – Arsenal
Ian Walker – Tottenham Hotspur
Gary Neville – Manchester United
Rob Jones – Liverpool
Tony Adams – Arsenal
Gary Pallister – Manchester United
Stuart Pearce – Nottingham Forrest
Steve Bould – Arsenal
John Beresford – Newcastle United
Jamie Redknapp – Liverpool
Robert Lee – Newcastle United
Gareth Southgate – Aston Villa
Steve McManaman – Liverpool
Steve Stone – Nottingham Forest
Dennis Wise – Chelsea
Nick Barmby – Middlesbrough

Les Ferdinand – Newcastle United
Teddy Sheringham – Tottenham Hotspur
Alan Shearer – Blackburn Rovers

The Norwegians play very deep and the back four in particular are very narrow. There is no space between midfield and defence. It is difficult to get over or through them, so we had to try and get them to come out to us. This is what we worked on in training. The problem is that they will not come past the halfway line. They wait to go into their trap, i.e. they wait for us to go and chase them, and that is what led to our previous problems with Norway.

We kept trying to go forward and chase the game, and so we left spaces. They just shot through and scored on the counter attack. That is what they are after, so we have to try and force them to make space.

NORWAY V ENGLAND 11 October 1995
The Ullevaal stadium
Attendance: 21,000
Norway: Thorstvedt, Loken, R Johnsen, Berg, Bjornebye, Flo, Bohinen, Leonhardsen (Solbakken 63), Fjørtoft (Brattbakk 80), Redkal, Jakobsen
England: Seaman, Neville, Pearce, Redknapp, Adams, Pallister, Barmby (Sheringham 67), Lee, Shearer, McManaman, Wise (Stone 67)
Result: 0–0
Referee: K–E Nilsson (Sweden)

Bearing in mind how Norway play we had to create space up the wings and try and take the full-backs on, but we weren't very successful. They have three players in midfield with Redkal holding. Both Bohinen and Leonhardsen get into the box to receive head downs from Fjørtoft. They have a left winger that raids and gives you problems wide, and they have a right winger Flo, who will come off the line and head down into the box.

However, in spite of this, I was very happy at the way we blocked Norway. They only got one chance when Bjornebye, the left-back, got a ball from a corner and cut back. The only reason this occurred was because Sheringham, on for Barmby, didn't stick close.

For the first time since I took over as England Coach I was concerned with the result rather than just seeing overall improvements in the team. It wasn't a home game and I needed to see how resolute our players could be away from home. I want the same as anyone else. I want to win, I want a good team performance and I want good individual performances. But I also need to see how the character of the team develops. I want to see how we react to intense pressure.

As I was watching the game I was pleased with our performance and how the players have picked things up and organized themselves. I thought David Seaman, along with the back four, put in an exceptional performance. We had a fifteen-minute period early on when we looked a little nervous, then we settled down. Jakobsen never got past Neville who, from a defensive point of view, had a very good game.

It wasn't 100 per cent entertaining. I was asked on television whether I was pleased with our performance and the answer was yes. Not because it was an entertaining match, it wasn't, but I wasn't asked that. I was asked if I was pleased with the overall performance. That is the difference between the two questions. I am looking for things that maybe the fans aren't.

We were, however, slaughtered by the Press. No one took into consideration that we drew away from home. But perhaps there are two sides to this: there is the professional viewpoint, and then the fans wanting entertainment and to see their country win. We didn't play a defensive game, we played Shearer and Barmby, even if Barmby was in a slightly deeper position like Beardsley. We had two wide players in Wise and McManaman, and in midfield we had Robert Lee who breaks forward a lot and, finally, in the holding position we had a footballer rather than a ball holder in Redknapp. So we really couldn't be accused of fielding a defensive side.

The problem is that Norway just make it difficult for you to find space. They want you to play in their half. That way they wait for you to make a mistake and then they go straight into a counter-attack.

If it had been a competitive game, rather than a friendly match, I would have said we were better keeping to the back and seeing whose nerve cracked first. In this case, they don't want to go over the halfway line, but if they don't move they aren't going to get the ball. Once they are over the halfway line we can get in amongst them and get at them. We did try and make space but it just wasn't that easy.

But I'm not scared of meeting them in the World Cup qualifying matches, as I would just hold out and force them to make a move. They want to play draughts, but I'd make sure they had to play a game of chess. It was interesting to see that when they played against Italy in the last World Cup the Norwegians needed only a draw to go through, and yet they failed to get it as they just weren't flexible enough. The Italians went 1–0 up and went down to ten men, but still Norway didn't change their system to take advantage of this. I thought this was their undoing. With an extra man they could have run Italy out of the game, forced a draw and possibly even won. They didn't react to the changes.

## Jean-Marc Bosman

After the Norwegian game came the contentious European Court ruling about Jean-Marc Bosman.

Bosman challenged the transfer fee structure by taking his past employers RFC Liege, plus the Belgian Federation and UEFA, to court over the fact that despite being at the end of his contract Liege were still demanding a transfer fee for him from French club US Dunkerque. He lost his chance of playing for Dunkerque when RFC Liege doubted the French club's ability to pay.

He won the case when the European Court of Justice ruled: 'The rules on transfers of players and the limits on the numbers of community players in inter-club matches are contrary to the Treaty of Rome.'

In essence I think that this is right. Over the last few years the chairmen of the clubs have been getting more unhappy with spiralling fees so I think it is a good thing if transfer fees are null and void when a contract is up. However, the same chairmen are all up in arms about it as they see their investments drop in value as the terms of the contract expires. But something has to happen to bring transfer fees down. I don't think players should be any different to anyone else. Why should they be worth a lot of money when they have served their contract out? I've had this opinion since I was on the PFA Committee as a player 28 years ago. Now I still feel the same as a National Team Coach.

The Professional Footballers' Association are trying to compromise, as are other interested parties. However, this ruling is the only chance the smaller clubs will have to be able to compete successfully in the market place, as they have the opportunity to pick up an out-of-contract player for no transfer fee.

Personally I think that players in the lower divisions should be part-time. I think this would enable the clubs to keep to a budget. They would still get the players, because players will need clubs. But the players would be better off in the long term under the 'no transfer fee once the contract has ended' rule. At the moment players in the second and third divisions earn about £300 a week. This isn't enough for the players to save much, so when they come to the end of their careers they haven't got anything to show for it in monetary terms. It means that their football careers have prevented them from progressing financially as some of their friends would have done. So your football career has in fact been a liability as you are ten or fifteen years older with no savings.

If, for example, they were driving a taxi for several hundred pounds a week, then playing part-time for a club and earning £250 a week, they could manage to save, so when their football careers are over they could still earn money from driving a taxi. From that point of view their football career has been of value to them and their skills as a footballer are a bonus. A lot of the Scandinavian countries have part-time players and they train in the evenings. I think this is why some of the Scandinavian countries have overtaken us in terms of progress. It doesn't mean they are less fit than our players, in fact in some cases they are fitter.

We are delaying inevitable change by funding smaller clubs who say they will repay their debts by selling a player for a lot of money. But most of the time this just doesn't happen. And at the end of their careers the majority of lower-division players are turfed out with no training for anything else and no savings.

The PFA will argue that the lower divisions are breeding grounds for the top clubs, but this will continue if the players go part-time. The scouts still go and watch non-league matches in the GM Conference league. We have quite a few players in the England team who started in non-league teams: Pearce, Flowers, Ian Wright. They will still come through.

By allowing clubs to struggle on full-time without adequate backing we are just burying our heads in the sand, and we should look at this problem a lot deeper.

However, my support of this development is not shared by

either Tom Pendry, the Shadow Minister for Sport, or by my own
chief executive, Graham Kelly. Tom's view is that the Government
has been somewhat laid-back in their response to the European
Court ruling: 'I am absolutely amazed at the complacent attitude
the Government has adopted over Bosman. At the very least it
should have gone to the court to argue for a transition period to
allow clubs to come to terms with the effects of the judgement.'

Apparently, the British Government refused to lobby the
court, whereas the German, Italian, French, Danish and other gov-
ernments did lobby them. Tom feels that this ruling will result in
many smaller and middle-income clubs abandoning their expen-
sive youth programmes, as the best players will be able to be
picked up for next to nothing by big clubs once their contracts
have run out. Well, I don't think it will be quite that bad, but the
fact remains that the smaller clubs will have to find alternative ways
of self-financing, such as part-time players.

As far as youth programmes go, the smaller clubs need to have
a very long-term view on this. It isn't something that will happen
overnight and the clubs can always give their young talent long
contracts, as some of the European clubs do. Plus you could
implement a policy of non-poaching as the Dutch do. Our youth
system must protect players at 15 and 17 years of age, as they do
now for younger players.

Graham Kelly is a little more circumspect over the whole affair.
His view is that things need to settle down and then there needs to
be a sensible discussion within UEFA. UEFA needs to, on the one
hand, negotiate with the players' unions, and then, if they can get
an agreement with the unions, they need to persuade the
European Commission that some form of transfer and compensa-
tion system is necessary. Graham says, 'I think there needs to be a
phasing of the transfer changes and a phasing of the three plus two
rule changes (which means, for example, that Scottish players will
no longer be foreigners in England), rather than an abolition of
them overnight, which is what some of our clubs seem to want.'

I don't think players can go and park themselves for a week
abroad and then come back on a free transfer. It makes a mockery
of the system. If you stop that but compromise on other aspects
you just complicate matters and leave yourself open to all kinds of
legal and professional problems. The policy should be simple and
clear-cut. These are things we've been pointing out for some time,

but it appears that neither the lawyers nor the politicians have taken much notice, although I do feel that Ian Sproat has been a good ally of ours over other issues.

**Kate Hoey**

Lo and behold, just as everything was settling down and I was beginning to think I could really concentrate on football, up pops Kate Hoey, intrepid Labour MP.

She declares an interest in sport, though Labour already have a Shadow Minister for Sport and Tourism in the shape of Tom Pendry. I last saw Ms Hoey sitting on Alan Sugar's table at the Football Writer's Dinner back in May, which was where I bumped into Jürgen Klinsmann. She was with the *Mirror*'s Harry Harris, Nick Hewer, Sugar's PR man, and Ken Bates, the Chairman of Chelsea Football Club.

Having had a little say about football matters before taking advantage of Parliamentary privilege, she stood up on 27 October 1995 in the House of Commons to make another speech. She addressed the issue of the Sheringham transfer (again without mentioning the outcome of the Companies Fraud Squad Enquiry). This time she referred to an invoice drawn up by a 'naughty knicker' company. Yet she cannot have checked the authenticity of these documents or even consulted with police acting on my complaint at the time. Once again she praised a journalist for 'producing' these documents: 'Because of the work by the *Daily Telegraph* and particularly Mihir Bose on this matter . . .'!

She also speculated on possible offences committed by me under Section 47 of the Financial Services Act 1986, relating to my purchase of Tottenham shares, implying criminal conduct and confessing that the investigation was not public knowledge. Once again, the media had a field day. Guess who were the key reporters?

Barely one month later the DTI announced that it would not proceed against me on any criminal charges.

Recently, Miss Hoey has said in public that she stands by everything she has said under Parliamentary privilege. Why does she not therefore, repeat her allegations in public?

I was pretty upset about her outburst and so I went and had a word with my old friend Tom Pendry. He confirmed that Ms Hoey was not following Labour Party policy in making her accusations and seemed to be baffled as to exactly why she has singled me out for attention. As he says, 'Kate Hoey has always had an interest in sport, but why she should be showing an interest in Terry is something I can't fathom.'

# CHAPTER TWENTY-FOUR

## THE EURO 96 ORGANIZATION

Glen Kirton thought that the media had gone way over the top in their criticism of the England team in Norway. I reassured him that things were on target as far as the team was concerned. I enquired if Glen had got all the various commercial contracts sorted out yet. He summarized for me, 'We have built up a Euro 96 commercial family of about forty companies who collectively have the exclusive right to associate themselves with the tournament. Each company has secured a number of marketing and commercial rights, including individual product exclusivity.

'The official sponsors of Euro 96 are: Canon, Carlsberg, Coca-Cola, Fujifilm, JVC, Mastercard, McDonald's, Philips, Snickers (Mars), Umbro and Vauxhall. The official suppliers, who have less of a financial input and therefore not quite such a high profile as the sponsors, are British Telecommunications, Castrol, Digital, Ladbrokes, Microsoft, Midland Bank, Sema Group (information systems providing TV graphics and press information). There are official products/services, i.e. those companies who will provide product at the tournament. Kelloggs is one of these. I wonder if that includes the team breakfast!

'There is also a group of "City Hosts", which will consist of local companies who will contribute to the event on a local basis. This includes the *Evening Standard* newspaper in London, Granada Television, and Northern Electric.

'Finally, there is a group of equipment suppliers: Cimara who specialize in the design, manufacture, distribution and management of corporate clothing; Harrod of Lowestoft, who will provide goalposts, nets and ground equipment; and London Communications, who are recognized as the foremost supplier and hirer of two-way radio communications systems, with depots throughout the UK.'

And what about the teams? What is their income likely to be?

'UEFA have allocated a maximum of ninety million Swiss Francs, which is to be divided amongst all the competing teams. It's true that the further you go the more you earn, but you also have to pay the players more!'

Security measures are being put into place. 'The ground work has been laid for the British police to exchange information with their European counterparts. If there is a group of troublemakers coming from a particular country, then the police from that country will tell our police. If the Government could prevent the troublemakers entering the country on the grounds of their past behaviour, then that would be great, but I doubt very much whether this would be legal. Anyway, even if they can't be turned away at point of entry then our police can keep them under constant surveillance.'

However, we don't want it to turn into a heavy-handed farce.

Glen laughed, 'No, at the World Cup in Italy in 1990, the police went mad in Rimini and arrested everyone with an English accent, including a British guy who was on holiday and had just nipped out for some cigarettes. He hadn't even gone for the football, and the next thing his wife knew he was phoning her from London to say he'd been put on a plane bound for England by the Italian police!

'But I don't think there will be major problems inside the stadiums. Each national football federation is responsible for the sale of its own tickets to its own supporters. They are going to be very careful. No one person can buy more than four tickets for a match and their name will be on the tickets.'

I wondered if there were any problems with the sponsors.

'No, generally that area seems to be going smoothly. The only problem is the eternal one of each sponsor thinking they have bought the world and not just the right to have an association with the event. They have rights that they have bought from ISL and we have to try and satisfy that. In certain cases there isn't the space in the grounds to deliver all the agreed things so you have to compromise. The biggest issue is the sponsors who have goods to supply in the grounds, for example, McDonald's. On the face of it McDonald's have exclusivity to supply every type of hot food, because that is their product. But we have had to ask McDonald's if they can supply the entire crowd. And the answer is no. We have an obligation from a safety point of view to supply all the fans with food. If someone wants to buy a burger and he has to go to a kitchen three miles down the road and queue with twenty thousand other people then that is clearly unacceptable. So we have had to insist that the ground management should be able to sell non-branded food.'

Visions of burger fights brought a smile to my face. It is astounding what one has to consider in putting on such a large event.

'Apart from worrying about burgers, things are going pretty smoothly. We are completing the television inspections and getting excellent co-operation from both BBC and ITV, who will show fifteen matches each. And both stations will televise the final. We are hoping the Queen will be there for the final, although we know she can't make the opening match as it is Derby Day. And I expect the Prime Minister will be present.'

# CHAPTER TWENTY-FIVE

## ALL THINGS SWEET AND NICE
## AND ON TO SWITZERLAND

In 1994 I was pleased to help launch the Snickers campaign to encourage youth football at grass roots level. Mars, who produce Snickers, devised this campaign to kit out kids with footballs and strips either free or at low cost in exchange for a certain number of Snickers wrappers. This was a huge success, with more than ten thousand schools and youth teams joining the programme, and over two thousand teams claiming free kit and equipment.

This is just the kind of initiative that helps kids at every age and level to get out and play football with their friends and school mates.

On Thursday, 19 October 1995 the relevant parties gathered at the Sports Café in London to launch a new campaign leading up to the European Championship finals. Mark Reid of Mars was there as was Malcolm Berry, chief executive of the English Schools FA, who rightly made the point that after the Prime Minister made his very important policy statement on the importance of school sport, with the emphasis on team games, they have been waiting for another announcement regarding the funding of the scheme. At the time of writing they are still waiting!

Without the sponsorship of companies like Mars, football at grass roots level would be in a somewhat sorry state. It's refreshing that not all big companies are interested only in sponsoring glamorous cup and international competitions. I am hoping that Mars will also go one step further and set up some regional soccer schools. There could then be regional competitions, with a national televised final. I'd like to see the joy being put back in the game at every level. If you can enjoy your football and win, then that's the ideal combination.

Mark said Mars were very happy with the way the campaign went in 1994, and that they've had a very positive feedback from the schools involved. Judging by the way the kids. at the launch were stuffing their bags with Snickers bars, it's obviously a marriage made in heaven! Mars, along with Green Flag, are also to take a major role in the senior team. By doing this they will be able to see how each level develops and how the game evolves towards the next century.

Talking about chocolate takes us smoothly on to the Swiss, producers of high-quality chocolate, who aren't bad at football either. They finished at the top of group three in the European Championship qualifiers and, unlike us, went to the World Cup in 1994.

### The Squad
David Seaman – Arsenal
Tim Flowers – Blackburn Rovers
Ian Walker – Tottenham Hotspur
Gary Neville – Manchester United
Rob Jones – Liverpool (went home on the Saturday due to injury)
Tony Adams – Arsenal
Steve Howey – Newcastle United
Gareth Southgate – Aston Villa
Gary Pallister – Manchester United
Stuart Pearce – Nottingham Forest
Graeme Le Saux – Blackburn Rovers
Trevor Sinclair – Queen's Park Rangers (went home Wednesday)
Steve Stone – Nottingham Forest
Jamie Redknapp – Liverpool
David Platt – Arsenal
Paul Gascoigne – Glasgow Rangers
Robert Lee – Newcastle United
Steve McManaman – Liverpool
Dennis Wise – Chelsea

Les Ferdinand – Newcastle United
Peter Beardsley – Newcastle United
Teddy Sheringham – Tottenham Hotspur
Alan Shearer – Blackburn Rovers

They have several very useful players. We knew that we would have to keep both Alain Sutter and Turkyilmaz under control. Alain Sutter is a left-sided player, very skilful and quick, so I realized I'd have to get someone on the wing to tie him down. Kubilay Turkyilmaz is a skilful, right-sided player who is very dangerous. He is a rather lazy player and lulls you into a false sense of security, then just as you think he's not in the game he pulls away, comes in on his left foot and scores.

Sforza is another very good footballer. He plays the holding role in the team, and is good at timing his runs. He supports the front players and is very good at set pieces. Sebastien Fournier is also a danger. He has very good vision, a good range of passing ability and also supports his front players very well.

I follow a pretty set routine when I am away with the team. It is a routine that has evolved over the past year or so and I am happy with the way we have all settled into it. To start with I try and leave the players at home as long as possible without making their requested arrival time too late in the evening.

My personal routine is to get up at 7.15am, and speak to various members of my staff, before leaving for training at 9.45am. I have a good-sized sitting room as well as a bedroom in my hotel suite, so I can have meetings in it, around a large boardroom table on which I place my tactics board. I use the board to play around with the tactics for the match as well as plot out that day's training session. I always have an idea in my head of how I want the team to play, then as training progresses, I start to fine-tune it and get it right for the actual match.

I also have a television and video in the room so I can watch matches of the opposition and then draw their tactical play on the board. This way I can start to see a clear pattern emerging of how they play and how we can best meet the challenges they provide.

About 9am Bryan Robson, Mike Kelly, Don Howe and Ted Buxton come into the room. We all discuss the plan for that day's training. At 9.20am David Davies comes in and briefs me on the content of the papers. I make a point of not reading the papers when I am away with the team. I think it is important for me to just keep my head clear and concentrate on the training session ahead. I may read the papers later in the day, but in the morning David just tells me the things I should know about. We decide what to do about any points that require reaction and then it's off to training.

On Saturday morning we leave at 9.30am for training and finish by midday as I like to let the players go home for the weekend. I think it is important to have this break: English teams have different habits to their European counterparts and are not used to being locked up in hotels before every league match.

I have found that I can do just as much with the players as I would do if they stayed all weekend. The players come back on Sunday evening about 9.30pm. This means they only eat a light meal after having eaten a large lunch with their families. The doctor and physios give me a report of any injuries, and we plan the next couple of days' training.

On match day we usually do set pieces. When we have a long time together before the European Championship finals start, I will probably practise set pieces after every training session. I have a few new themes on free kicks and corner kicks, which I want to keep secret until the finals. I know that the opposition managers study us and I want to give them a few surprises when we start playing for real. So far I've kept things fairly simple. We knew the Swiss play a 4-4-2 with the slight difference that Sutter plays left wing coming into midfield. Therefore we practised on keeping compact and getting the ball quickly so as not to give them any time. This worked very well, particularly as Sheringham was drawing their left-back Quentin in deep, and Stone was able to make the most of the space left behind him.

ENGLAND V SWITZERLAND 15 November 1995
Wembley stadium
Attendance: 29,874
England: Seaman, Neville, Pallister, Adams, Pearce, Lee, Gascoigne, Redknapp (Stone 7), McManaman, Shearer, Sheringham
Switzerland: Pascolo, Hottiger, Quentin (Vega 82), Henchoz, Geiger, Fournier (Wolf 69), Sutter (Grassi 80), Ohrel, Knup, Sforza, Turkyilmaz

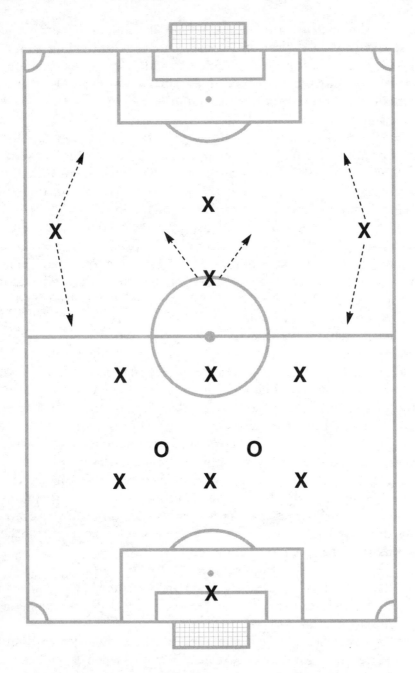

**England's formation versus Colombia, Norway and Switzerland
playing 2 forwards against opposition**

◄---- Shows player movement

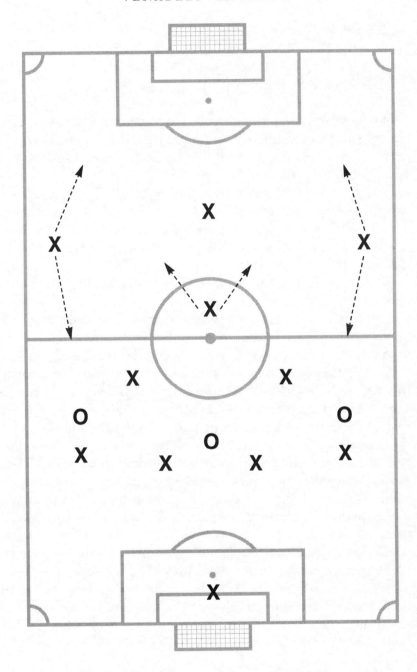

**England's formation versus Colombia, Norway and Switzerland
playing 3 forwards against opposition**

◄---- Shows player movement

Result: 3–1
Scorers: Knup 41
        Pearce 45, Sheringham 56, Stone 78
Referee: S Puhl (Hungary)

I was very pleased with the way we played. In fact, I have been
pleased since Colombia. We didn't get the goals against Colombia
that we did against Switzerland, but we played as well against them
as we did in this match.

I think we played some very good football. They played with
two strikers up front, a winger and three in midfield, which helped
us as I didn't have to get my centre-half out to cover them. If the
opposition play with five in the midfield then I have to pull my
full-backs forward or wide.

They only had one wide player, Alain Sutter. They had a problem in that their left-back, Quentin, didn't want to watch
Sheringham. So Teddy's job was to go towards him, draw him
back and leave space for Lee, or Steve Stone, as it turned out to be,
to get down the side and get the crosses over to Shearer.

By creating space behind Quentin, we gave ourselves a chance
to score. I thought Redknapp did very well before he got injured
and I was looking forward to Lee playing a slighter wider role. We
were lucky in that Stone came on and did such a good job.

Gazza is getting better, but he needs to get a bit more disciplined and not complicate matters. Some people asked why I
warmed up Peter Beardsley during the last few minutes of the
game. Well, it was to give Gazza a warning that I wanted him to
stay in midfield and just concentrate on what he was supposed to
be doing.

I only made a couple of half-time points. I wanted
McManaman to take on the right-back on the outside (even if he
wasn't successful), just to unsettle the Swiss defender so that the
next time he wanted to cut inside he'd create more room for himself. I also wanted Neville to stay tucked up to Adams. He was
drifting a bit wide and allowing Turkyilmaz to get in between him
and Adams.

Having corrected that, we didn't have problems with balls
going down the outside of us in the second half.

I came off the pitch feeling very satisfied. We have reached the
turning point and are firmly on the right road to the European

Championship finals. However, I think we will see a very different Switzerland in the summer. They have a new manager, Artur Jorge, who is very much a European man. He speaks six languages and will inject a new flavour of optimism into the team. At Wembley, it has to be said, the Swiss team were without sight of their squad choices: Chapuisat, Yakin, Vogel, Thuler, Subiat, Zuberbuhier, Herr and Bickel. I think we will see a different, more solid team in June.

# CHAPTER TWENTY-SIX

## THE SECOND EUROPEAN MANAGERS' MEETING AND PORTUGAL AT WEMBLEY

By December the number of managers still involved in Europe had dwindled to one – Frank Clark of Nottingham Forest.

It is a sad and sorry state, and a session was needed to take a look at how we can improve performance.

The managers were all very open about their problems. Graham Kelly was present, and enquired if the FA could help in relation to timing. He wanted to know how we could rearrange fixtures to give the clubs time to prepare, and then maybe some time afterwards to recoup before having to go on and play another league match. The meeting was really about organization and practical details and was an important step in increasing communication between the FA and the professional side of the game. Our European counterparts have the help of their national football associations in terms of time given to prepare. We need to catch up and do the same.

Graham said, 'There can be no doubt that our clubs have under-achieved in Europe this season. In fact, apart from a couple of successes, the record of our clubs since the European ban was lifted has not been good.

'We feel it is important that we bend over backwards to help our clubs so that they don't go into important European matches with one hand tied behind their backs. The role of the FA is to help football and promote it at every level.'

The need for more time was one thing that all the managers were in agreement about. Therefore, the FA will make two recommendations to the Premier League. The first is that weekend fixtures should be postponed on request to allow four days' preparation before European matches, and the second is that teams competing in Europe should be given a bye in the second round of the Coca-Cola Cup.

The twenty Premier League chairmen must vote on the plans, which Graham sees as the starting point of a longer-term strategy to re-establish English football as a major force in Europe.

Taking tactics and strategy into consideration, I think Nottingham Forest are still in Europe because they have been a bit more careful than the others. They have adopted the cagey attitude of not giving goals away and not going all out to score. If you leave your defence light of players when you're attacking, these teams are so good at counter-attacking, you'll very quickly be a goal down. Frank did admit that they have been more cautious in their European matches than they have in the Premier League.

## The FA Cup Draw

This was the first time we had a bit of a glitz in the proceedings for the draw, and I think it worked very well. The FA Cup is still the most prestigious national club competition in Europe, and why shouldn't we make a bit of song and dance about it?

I think for the sponsors, the television coverage worked very well. I found it easy to work with Denis Law, we have a good bit of banter going between us. I think this would also work well on the radio.

The only really big criticism I had of the proceedings was the camera angles. The front row of players – Andy Cole, Les Ferdinand and Dave Watson – was electric. I have never seen so much fear on the faces of players, not even in the dressing room before a big match. The expectancy was amazing, but there was no camera to capture their expressions. You would have thought that when Chelsea came out of the bag, the camera would have been on Mark Hughes, before moving straight over to Les Ferdinand when Newcastle were drawn. I thought that was a weak link.

I think it could develop into a great programme maybe something like the Lottery broadcast, where the draw is just the climax of an entertaining show.

## Lead-up to England v Portugal

The Portuguese are very skilled and play with a packed midfield, which means we had to be ready to wear them down in that area and get through to score. Ted went and watched the Republic of Ireland play Portugal in the European Championship qualifiers and here is an extract from his report on the main players:

Luis Pinto plays in a Sheringham-type position just behind Domingos. He looks to get forward, pushes right up, looks to play in, to get put in, and he gets crosses over. He can look a bit suspect when pressured, and gave the ball away quite a few times.

Rui Costa, their playmaker, is a quality player. He's right-sided, well balanced and comfortable on both feet. He has good vision and passing ability both long and short. He has the ability to strike balls on target from distances. He's one of the men to watch!

Striker Domingos has good ball control and turns well and will be a danger to our defence. Another very useful player is Figo. He breaks well and loses his marker, and also makes good runs to support the forward positions. It seems he has pace when he is breaking into the attacking third.

I think that Luis Pinto, Ricardo Sa Figo (who plays for Barcelona) and Rui Costa are probably the main men we will have to watch. When they break into the attacking third they look to shoot, but then drag the ball back on to their other foot to get an extra yard.

As a quality side Portugal play out from the back and through the midfield. They push their wide men in, and look to get them into areas where they play into the front players; to get the modified players breaking into space in the attacking third.

Defensively, Portugal can look suspect at times when they are squeezing up; they can look very square, and it should be possible to get by them by passes aimed to get in behind the full-backs, especially behind the left full-back, who tends to cave in when under pressure.

They play their full-backs fairly wide with the two centre-halves, with one just in front of the other. This is similar to the role Mauro da Silva played in the World Cup for Brazil.

## The Squad

David Seaman – Arsenal
Tim Flowers – Blackburn Rovers
Ian Walker – Tottenham Hotspur
Gary Neville – Manchester United
Rob Jones – Liverpool
Tony Adams – Arsenal
Steve Howey – Newcastle United
Gareth Southgate – Aston Villa
Stuart Pearce – Nottingham Forest
Graeme Le Saux – Blackburn Rovers
Steve Stone – Nottingham Forest
Dennis Wise – Chelsea
Paul Gascoigne – Glasgow Rangers
Steve McManaman – Liverpool
Trevor Sinclair – Queen's Park Rangers
Peter Beardsley – Newcastle United
Nick Barmby – Middlesbrough
Les Ferdinand – Newcastle United
Alan Shearer – Blackburn Rovers

We only had one day to prepare for the match against Portugal, and quite frankly it wasn't long enough. By the time you've absorbed the injuries and contacted substitute players, and then got down to Burnham Beeches, there is hardly any time to work with the players and achieve the type of play you want from them.

Portugal do have good tactical players and not surprisingly they play like the Brazilians. They are a good side and I think they will finish in the top five or six in Euro 96. As challengers to Italy and Germany, Spain and Portugal are coming along fast. They are both young teams who have been playing together quite a long time and are very talented. Then of course there is also Russia, who are very strong.

Against Portugal I aimed to have four at the back, with a full-back or even central defender pushed in to help the midfield. I had Le Saux in mind again. He is a very valuable player because he can play in left-back, left-half or left-wing position. This high level of flexibility is very important to England and I was very disappointed when he was injured. It was a big blow for us as we need versatile players of his calibre. I want to experiment and get the combination right between Shearer and Sheringham, or between Sheringham and Ferdinand. Shearer, Sheringham or Ferdinand are my first-choice front players and I want them to have as much experience of playing together as possible.

I went to see Chelsea v Newcastle on the Saturday before the game. Many England players play for these two teams and so I was able to look at several possibilities. Barton is on the edge of the team and a very good player.

I asked a couple of the youth team players to join the squad at Burnham Beeches. This is to continue my policy of letting the youngsters get experience of what it's like in the senior squad, and to start to get to know how it works. John O'Connor from Everton and Chris Holland from Newcastle came down. I've had the chance to experiment with more players than I initially envisaged.

Looking back, the first match against Denmark was a honeymoon period: I had all the players I wanted available to me. After that I've had to chop and change around, which I must say has been good for me as I've had the chance to experiment. In many ways it would have been disastrous if I had had all the players fit and then a big injury problem on the eve of the European Championship finals. This is the best way round as I've learnt how to adapt. This time I had Platt, Lee and Redknapp out. I could have gone outside the group, to get two wide players, but then I would have had to have an extra midfield player. Instead, I decided to vary the type of play to suit the players available. I decided to use this game as if it were a European Championship final match, and I had to use the players in the squad.

I decided to have Stone on the wing, with Gazza and Barmby tucked into midfield. That left Ferdinand and Shearer up front with Barmby just behind them. Barmby could play balls out to either side or up the middle to ensure the strikers were adequately serviced. We had the usual back four.

ENGLAND V PORTUGAL Tuesday 12 December
Wembley stadium
Attendance: 28,592
England: Seaman, Neville, Pearce (Le Saux 79), Wise (Southgate 79), Adams, Howey, Barmby (McManaman 79),

Gascoigne, Shearer, Ferdinand (Beardsley 63), Stone.
Portugal: Neno, Carlos Secretario, Dimas, Costa, Couto, Sousa (Alves 45), Figo (Dominguez 45), J Pinto (Dani 60), S Pinto, Helder, Folha (Pedro 7).
Result: 1–1
Scorers: Stone 44
        Alves 58
Referee: R Pedersen (Norway)

I was very pleased with England in the first half. I thought Portugal were one of the best teams we had played. Fernando Couto, their captain, was excellent. Their similarity to Brazil goes deeper than the same touches and sheer skill. Portugal and Brazil share the same language and have a similar culture and outlook on life. They have a lot of good young players coming through, players who have played at international youth level, or in the Under-21 team. This means they are now reaping the benefits of this long-term development plan.

I think we deserved the goal as we were the better side. I feel we could have got a second goal if our touch and our attacking play in the last third had been on form. We were a little off.

When we came back on to the pitch in the second half, Portugal had changed their team slightly and made a couple of substitutions, Alves for Sousa and Dominguez for Figo. That changed their style and they gave us problems for the next twenty or twenty-five minutes. Then we came back and I think we could have scored in the last fifteen minutes.

Southgate came on and played very well. He got stuck in and got straight down to it, and I really liked his attitude. That is exactly the type of attitude I want to see from an England international player. He is showing a lot of promise and stands a chance of being in the squad for the finals. I'll have to see how the squad shapes up in terms of injuries. As I am limited to 21 players I will have to choose players who are flexible and adaptable, rather than just specialists. I haven't got the luxury of being able to pick a cover for every position, so I will have to have several players who can cover a couple of positions.

But all in all, I was pleased with our performance and things are developing along the lines I want. I want to see Redknapp back and I would like to be able to play in the style I have mapped out

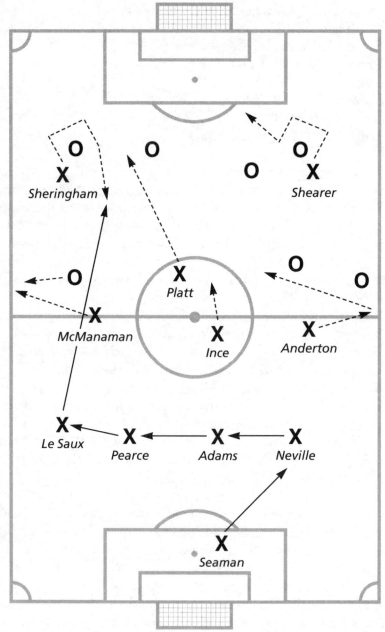

This time the ball to Shearer is not possible. The ball is played across the back four. Same principal as before but played on the other side.

**England's set play in movement to create space**

◄----- Shows player movement       ◄——— Shows ball movement

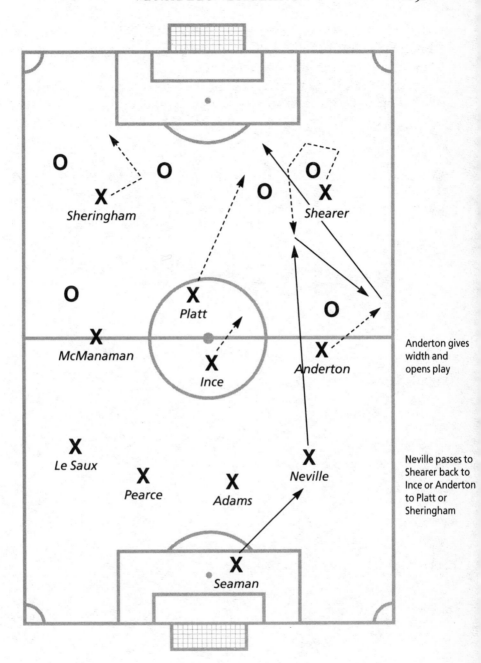

**England's set play in movement to create space**

◀---- Shows player movement     ◀—— Shows ball movement

if all my first choice players are available. I think it is wise to create space in a game. Only by doing that will you be able to open it up and create opportunities to score goals.

We are on target for next summer. I look forward to going to Birmingham for the Euro 96 draw next Sunday.

# CHAPTER TWENTY-SEVEN

## CUP DRAWS

Well, this sure ain't easy! But then to be fair there is no such thing as an easy team these days. In our group for the World Cup will be Italy, Poland, Georgia and Moldova.

The Italian team speaks for itself, three times winners of the World Cup and a finalist in the 1994 World Cup of America. Italy are a prime example of a great, modern team. Over the years they have redefined themselves and adapted to new conditions. Just when you think the team is getting a bit old and maybe will suffer a lull for a few years, they find yet more young talent. It just seems to flow out of the valleys like the wine.

The latest to take the country by storm is Alessandro Del Piero, the youngster who has usurped Baggio at Juventus. Like Baggio he has the same consummate skill and ease of play that makes a great champion. There are many world-class players in the Italian team. Ravanelli is very good, Paolo Maldini is one of the best defenders in the world, and Lazio star Giuseppe Signori is a dangerous threat in attack.

Although the Italians are the stars of the show, the other teams in our group are not to be taken lightly. Poland are an old adversary of ours and although they are not as strong as they were, I think they'll try and develop a younger team. They could pick players from the Olympic Squad, which will mean quite a few unknown players for us to play against.

Although Georgia and Moldova are relative newcomers, they have vast experience as a lot of their players were in the old Russian team. Several teams have found out just how good these teams are when they have met them in recent qualifying matches.

I aim to win the group, but if we don't I would hope for a second place and the chance of a play-off. I have to say that I would have preferred to have seven groups of seven teams. Then the two top teams would have qualified and the other two places could have been decided through play-offs by the third place teams.

I suppose it wouldn't make that much difference except you'd have another couple of games, which could have been good experience. However FIFA decided on this system and that's that.

## My contract

The silly season is well under way with everyone blowing hot and cold about a possible new contract. I will be sitting down to discuss terms with the FA in the first week of January. As I am writing this it is December, two days before the European Championship finals draw in Birmingham and the countdown to the biggest sporting tournament staged in England since the 1966 World Cup.

I am very excited by the prospect of being National Coach of the host nation and I am giving everything to prepare the best team possible, but I have to have the full support of the FA. Sir Bert Millichip and Graham Kelly have always been extremely supportive of me and my work, but several others, most notably Noel White, have chosen to discuss their thoughts about me in the Press. I have to say that I would prefer it if members of the FA would have the courtesy of letting me know what they think in person. I would respect someone who called me and said, 'Look I have been asked to make a comment in the Press, and I feel I have to say x, y, z, but I wanted to let you know first.' Even if it's negative I can respect someone's honesty in following their line of thought, even if it doesn't coincide with mine. But I am fed up with people who back-bite and snipe at me from within the organization I work for, without feeling able to tell me first what they think.

So the answer about me renewing my contract with the FA is that yes, I would love to lead England to France for the World Cup in 1998, and beyond. However, there is no way I am continuing in my present position without the full support of everyone concerned at the FA. Therefore, as I write this, it looks extremely doubtful that I will be continuing on as England Coach past this summer's European Championship.

## The European Championship Draw

Having been concentrating on getting the team right, it wasn't until I arrived in Birmingham on Saturday afternoon, 16 December, that I realized the countdown to Euro 96 had seriously begun. The place was buzzing with excitement, and I started to feel the anticipation and expectations of the people involved in the event.

However, I was feeling far from happy due to articles in several Saturday papers which reported some quotes from Noel White, Chairman of the International Committee. For some time Noel White had been fairly vocal through the press in expressing doubts about my suitability to continue as England Coach after the European Championship finals. The Saturday *Daily Mail* had some more criticisms from him.

The previous day as I recorded my thoughts about the World Cup draw, I was feeling pretty bullish about the future. Late in October Toots and I had discussed my position as England Coach over dinner one night. We had come to the conclusion that if you are the England Coach then you should see the job through to the World Cup, which quite frankly would have been the highlight of my career. I am very happy with the way the team is coming together and in another two years I thought we would once again, be a great side.

I thought there could be a chance that certain members of the FA International Committee would stop criticizing me in the Press. Both Toots and I felt very strongly that the FA should speak with one voice, and that the people who spoke to the Press should be Graham Kelly and David Davies, but it seemed impossible to co-ordinate this. Now there had to be a showdown between me and Noel White.

Graham Kelly knew this, and he was waiting for me in the reception area of the hotel. We went to my room to discuss the matter of Noel White and Ian Stott, who had also made public comments casting doubts on my future. At this juncture I told Graham that I didn't want to continue as England Coach unless I had 100 per cent support not only from him and Sir Bert but from everyone on the International Committee, and in the FA, and I wouldn't consider waiting until after the tournament before nego-tiating a contract. I agreed to meet with White, and this was arranged for the Sunday. Quite frankly, I wanted to see him on his own and thrash things out with only the two of us present, but Graham and Sir Bert felt that they should be there too.

I duly confronted Noel White and told him that I could understand the fact that he had comments to make about me, but I would have preferred it if he had made them directly to me rather than my having to read about them over breakfast along with millions of other people. He then denied that he had made the comments. I replied that in that case the matter was very simple. 'Could you put a statement out in the morning that says not only were you misquoted but that you didn't actually say anything about me at all?'

Sir Bert agreed that a statement of this kind would be helpful. But then White capitulated somewhat and admitted that he had said, 'I will support Terry until 1996.' This, of course, was completely different from saying nothing. Basically what he meant was that he wouldn't dream of giving me a contract until Euro 96 was over.

I then said, 'But that was what was quoted in the papers, so you did say it!' He replied, 'But you haven't had any competitive matches.' I pointed out, 'I've had competitive matches all my life. I was in Barcelona for three years – if they aren't competitive matches I don't know what are!'

But even forgetting that, if I remain as Coach to the end of Euro 96 the new man won't take over before that and so he wouldn't · have any competitive matches either. In fact, he wouldn't have had any matches at all!

I told White I didn't do auditions. He clearly wanted to watch the horse going over the winning line before having a bet on it. I added that this wasn't good enough. I don't know of any chairman who, if he valued his manager, would let him come to the end of his contract before renewing it. No one who wanted his manager to continue would risk losing him by leaving the agreement of the contract so late. I added that he obviously had his doubts about me and that the best thing was to leave it, but that if they waited until the end of the competition before deciding whether to renew my contract, they wouldn't have any time to find anyone else. Within a month of Euro 96 ending, the World Cup qualifying matches start. How can we expect to look to the future with this kind of dithering going on? It really does amaze me. I told them that the Danish coach, Richard Møller-Nielsen, is off to

Finland after Euro 96. He has already signed for the Finnish and the Danes have already appointed a new coach to take over for the World Cup qualifying matches. That is planning ahead and normal practice in modern European football.

Anyway, looking at things realistically, which seems to be an impossibility for the FA, if I didn't sign a new contract until after Euro 96, there would be all sorts of rumours and counter-rumours circulating that would just serve to undermine my preparations for the team. The media would have a field day while the FA would be talking to possible new coaches and I would be talking to possible new employers, all behind each other's backs. What kind of situation is that to create at a time when we are trying to rebuild a shattered image and bring some glory back to the England football team?

I then simply said to Noel White that Graham Kelly knew my position and my insistence on having full support, so if it wasn't there it would be best if I left the job of England Coach. I then got up and walked out, leaving the three of them to chew things over.

Just before Christmas I had a meeting with Graham Kelly and he asked me if I still felt the same. I told him I did. He asked me if I'd made my mind up, and I said yes. I was going away in January for a week's holiday with Toots to Oman. Graham asked me to think about it during that week.

From this I gathered that things may change in my absence and that there would be some work done behind the scenes to ascertain exactly who thought what about me and why. But when I returned from holiday, nothing had been done, the situation was static and so my decision was unchanged. Graham and I then announced my decision to the Press to let everyone know. And that was that.

I have subsequently spoken to Noel White and Ian Stott and there are no hard feelings on either side. The FA decided to honour my present contract, and I remain completely committed to the European Championship finals. I thought it quite reasonable to wish each other luck and a good Euro 96. However, as Noel White is a director of Liverpool Football Club, I think we can safely assume that I won't be offered the job of managing Liverpool.

Back in Birmingham we had an official dinner on the Saturday evening, which was attended by all the team delegations as well as the UEFA boxes. I got the chance to meet up with some old friends from my Barcelona days, and meet some new faces. One face I was sad to see wasn't present was that of Jack Charlton. It won't seem like a big international tournament without the Irish, and I wish Jack all the best in the future. He has done a tremendous job for Irish football and for Ireland. I thought the Irish put up a good fight against the Dutch in the play-off at Anfield, but the Dutch team were just unbeatable. A class side, I am sure Holland will do well in the finals.

I bumped into Peter Lee, who runs the Football Trust. The Football Trust was founded in 1975, through an initiative by the pools companies Littlewoods, Vernons and Zetters, and it is helping the game at all levels – from providing kit for school teams, pitches and changing rooms for amateur football, to safety and improvement work throughout the game right up to the national stadiums.

The Trust's priority is to allocate the reduction in pool betting duty funds to help clubs redevelop or move to new grounds. Grants totalling some £130 million have been distributed throughout the game. All the host stadiums for Euro 96 have had substantial grant assistance: Aston Villa, £2.8m; Leeds United, £2.18m; Liverpool, £2.7m; Manchester United, £1.6m; Nottingham Forest, £2.13; Newcastle United, £2.85m; Sheffield Wednesday, £2.8m; and Wembley Stadium, £2m.

I was very busy on the Sunday morning, as being coach of the host nation, I was in demand from the various participating countries' media. But two o'clock came round very quickly and I sat in the front row of the auditorium alongside the other national coaches.

The four seeded teams were England, as host nation, Denmark, as the reigning title holders, and Germany and Spain, on the basis of their results in the qualifying competitions for the 1994 World Cup and the 1996 European Championship. The remaining twelve final-round participants were put into a second draw pot.

I was impressed with the show that Alec McGivan organized. It was simple but effective. Children dressed up in the different team colours and said hello in the native languages of the participating countries. It was a very nice touch, a good way of communicating a message to everyone. Too often these events become boring as the host nation rabbits on in its native language and everyone else is left looking at the ceiling or trying to follow the simultaneous translation. The theme song sung by Simply Red, with a choral backing, was a reflection of our 'we're all together' philosophy, which promotes the ability of football to unite countries and bring them together in enjoying the entertainment of one of the world's most popular sports.

Then came the moment when our opposition would be revealed. It was all very quiet, then we drew Scotland in our group and the auditorium erupted as the implications of a home nations match sunk in. I was delighted. I'd wanted to reinstate an annual England v Scotland match for some time, and here it was being handed to us as part of a prestigious international tournament.

Someone asked if it would be a help to have Gazza playing for Rangers, as he could provide us with useful information about Scottish players. Yes, it will be, but we mustn't forget that a lot of Scottish players play for English clubs, and they will know a lot about us.

And, of course, we know all about the Netherlands – a side of exceptionally talented young players – and Switzerland who we had just played prior to the draw even if they now have a new coach, who will stamp his own style on the team.

I spoke to Graham Kelly soon after the draw. Like all of us at the FA, he's excited at the prospect of hosting the European Championship finals and putting on a good show for all the fans and visitors. He thought that the draw gave us a good chance of progressing. He does feel that with the progress England has made under me (thanks for the vote of confidence), we have a good chance of making it to the later stages.

I asked him what impression he would like visitors to be left with. He replied, 'Anything that approaches that which I was left with after the 1994 World Cup in America. That was such a fiesta, with the fans turning it into a carnival of colour and celebration. I think we can recapture that and get the same buzz of excitement, and that will provide the fans with a vivid memory to return home with. Our main aim is to stimulate interest in football in the long term. We want kids to feel the same kind of enthusiasm we felt after 1966. In the short term it won't be a financially lucrative tournament for us, but we have to think of the long-term advantages. A lot of the money UEFA makes is ploughed back in to European

# EURO 96
## FINAL DRAW

| Group A | | Group B | | Group C | | Group D | |
|---|---|---|---|---|---|---|---|
| Wembley | Villa Park | Elland Road | St James' Park | Old Trafford | Anfield | Hillsborough | City Ground |
| London | Birmingham | Leeds | Newcastle | Manchester | Liverpool | Sheffield | Nottingham |
| 1 ENGLAND | | 1 SPAIN | | 1 GERMANY | | 1 DENMARK | |
| 2 SWITZERLAND | | 2 BULGARIA | | 2 CZECH REPUBLIC | | 2 PORTUGAL | |
| 3 NETHERLANDS | | 3 ROMANIA | | 3 ITALY | | 3 TURKEY | |
| 4 SCOTLAND | | 4 FRANCE | | 4 RUSSIA | | 4 CROATIA | |

| | | | | | | | |
|---|---|---|---|---|---|---|---|
| Saturday 8th June | 1 | A1 | England – Switzerland | A2 | Wembley | 3:00 |
| Sunday 9th June | 2 | B1 | Spain – Bulgaria | B2 | Elland Road | 2:30 |
| | 3 | C1 | Germany – Czech Republic | C2 | Old Trafford | 5:00 |
| | 4 | D1 | Denmark – Portugal | D2 | Hillsborough | 7:30 |
| Monday 10th June | 5 | A3 | Netherlands – Scotland | A4 | Villa Park | 4:30 |
| | 6 | B3 | Romania – France | B4 | St James' Park | 7:30 |
| Tuesday 11th June | 7 | C3 | Italy – Russia | C4 | Anfield | 4:30 |
| | 8 | D3 | Turkey – Croatia | D4 | City Ground | 7:30 |
| Thursday 13th June | 9 | A2 | Switzerland – Netherlands | A3 | Villa Park | 7:30 |
| | 10 | B2 | Bulgaria – Romania | B3 | St James' Park | 4:30 |
| Friday 14th June | 11 | C2 | Czech Republic – Italy | C3 | Anfield | 7:30 |
| | 12 | D2 | Portugal – Turkey | D3 | City Ground | 4:30 |
| Saturday 15th June | 13 | A4 | Scotland – England | A1 | Wembley | 3:00 |
| | 14 | B4 | France – Spain | B1 | Elland Road | 6:00 |
| Sunday 16th June | 15 | C4 | Russia – Germany | C1 | Old Trafford | 3:00 |
| | 16 | D4 | Croatia – Denmark | D1 | Hillsborough | 6:00 |
| Tuesday 18th June | 17 | A4 | Scotland – Switzerland | A2 | Villa Park | 7:30 |
| | 18 | B4 | France – Bulgaria | B2 | St James' Park | 4:30 |
| | 19 | A3 | Netherlands – England | A1 | Wembley | 7:30 |
| | 20 | B3 | Romania – Spain | B1 | Elland Road | 4:30 |
| Wednesday 19th June | 21 | C4 | Russia – Czech Republic | C2 | Anfield | 7:30 |
| | 22 | D4 | Croatia – Portugal | D2 | City Ground | 4:30 |
| | 23 | C3 | Italy – Germany | C1 | Old Trafford | 7:30 |
| | 24 | D3 | Turkey – Denmark | D1 | Hillsborough | 4:30 |
| Saturday 22nd June | 25 | | 1B – 2A | | Anfield | 6:30 |
| | 26 | | 2B – 1A | | Wembley | 3:00 |
| Sunday 23rd June | 27 | | 1C – 2D | | Old Trafford | 3:00 |
| | 28 | | 2C – 1D | | Villa Park | 6:30 |
| Wednesday 26th June | 29 | | W25 – W28 | | Old Trafford | 4:00 |
| | 30 | | W26 – W27 | | Wembley | 7:30 |
| Sunday 31st June | 31 | | Final | | Wembley | 7:00 |

football, and will serve to promote the game during the coming years.'

Graham was also very positive about a project developed in conjunction with the National Union of Teachers and supported by Canon UK and Philips Electronics, to promote interest in Euro 96, and also help kids to be informed about other European countries.

We have produced a booklet for teaching purposes, which takes the kids through Europe and gives them information about the forty-eight countries who participated in the Championship. Each country has a section on its history, geography and economy, and so is invaluable for helping the kids to understand how other people live, and their philosophies on life.

We've devised a competition which runs in several categories, like writing a poem, a song or an essay, for instance, and the participating school has to choose a category and then enter. It is open to primary schools, special schools, secondary schools and sixth-form colleges.

Initially, the competition will be judged regionally, then the forty regional winners will qualify for the national adjudication to be held at Wembley stadium in late May 1996. The winners will attend the European Championship Final on 30 June.

Of course, after the initial excitement of an England–Scotland match, the main debate turned to security. The Department of Heritage has this well in hand. Once it was known which matches would be played where, a concentrated campaign was initiated, whereby the specific police representatives of each country exchanged information with the relevant English police force. So the Dutch police are liaising with the Metropolitan and Birmingham police, and the German police with the Manchester and Liverpool forces.

We have a lot of experience in this area, and the Government is handling the situation with sensitivity and intelligence. They have managed to bring together groups of people that the FA would have found difficult to organize. For example, the Government has managed to arrange a special fast-flow channel to ensure that the teams and the people involved in the tournament will get a smooth welcome into the country. They also have plans to reduce the roadworks and motorway cones to a minimum! (It's a pity we can't continue this after the event!) One problem has been that with the deregulation and privatization of many services it is difficult to talk to one body about a specific problem. When we wanted to discuss the needs of the fans with the coach operators it was impossible to get all the representatives together, as there are so many coach companies.

The Government has produced a booklet on the finals for all the embassies, so they can provide information to fans from their countries. The brochure goes through the history of the European Championship and then on to how the event will be organized in England. They have a section dedicated to the various host stadiums, calling them 'Theatres of Dreams', which I think is a great expression. These grounds are places where our dreams can be realized or dashed, and a really fantastic match can lift your spirits for a long time afterwards, even entering the annuals of historic record.

The most important thing is for Euro 96 to inject enthusiasm and interest in the game amongst young kids.

# CHAPTER TWENTY-EIGHT

## REFLECTIONS

I escaped to Oman in January for a few days rest and relaxation with Toots. 1995 had been quite a year for both of us, some happy times and some sad times. It was good to recoup my energy and contemplate the months to come. Toots has seen us go through highs and lows and she personally finds several aspects of my job and life very frustrating. The first is obviously the behaviour of certain elements of the media. The second is the matter of finding a judge for the many court cases that are coming my way who, with all the media coverage that I generate, hasn't got an even slightly clouded opinion of me, after all the relentless, negative coverage in certain sections of the press.

It all leads to added pressure on us. As Toots says, 'People often say to me, "How do you cope with the hassle? It must be like living in a nightmare." My answer is always the same: "You just get on with it, what else can you do? It becomes part of your life, you just want to clear your name and you keep going until you do." I'm sure when it's all over, we'll ask ourselves how on earth we coped. But at the time you just do.'

I am very lucky to have Toots, and we have become even closer during this last three years. Shakespeare said: 'Thus conscience doth make cowards of us all.' It's so true. When your conscience is clear you can be incredibly brave.

Now the European Championship finals are just around the corner. In January the Football League signed a television contract that Graham Kelly believes is important in that it will buy some valuable time for the second and third division clubs. The contract is very lucrative compared to what they've had for the last four years. It's an increase from £9 million to £25 million a year, and this gives us all some space to consider the future of the second and third division clubs. The issue of whether these clubs continue with full-time football or become part-timers will have to be considered within the lifetime of this contract. At the moment the ninety-two clubs are keeping afloat, but there certainly will not be enough money to keep them all going for ever, especially considering that the bulk of the money will go to the First Division clubs.

However, the moment you start thinking of part-time football, the lower division clubs get huffy and don't like the thought of not participating full-time. Maybe on this issue the Bosman ruling will concentrate everyone's minds.

Graham has three New Year resolutions, three wishes for 1996. The first one is to score the winning goal in a Cup Final, but he admits this isn't very realistic. He did play football, but not professionally. His managers often said of him: 'I have tried you in every position but never with any satisfaction!'

His second (and most important) wish is for England to do well in Euro 96, and for the tournament to run smoothly and be successful. We both believe that a triumphant Euro 96 will see the rebirth of football from the grass roots to the highest grade, and this has to be good for the kids and for the professionals.

His last wish is for Blackpool to win promotion! This seems even more unrealistic than scoring the winning goal in a Cup Final. We have more chance of winning Euro 96 and the World Cup in 1998!

I have now been England Coach for twenty-four months. Here is Graham's assessment so far:

'Terry is making good progress. He is getting younger players like Stone, McManaman, Redknapp and Barmby through to the senior team and making them understand the requirements of being part of an international team. He is moulding them into a successful unit. I see this as a layman, but I believe the vast majority of professional coaches who I talk to see it like this as well. They think he is steering the team along the right lines.

'He came to us with a glowing reputation and I think that has been confirmed. He was known as a strategist, a tactician, and a gifted coach who was experienced, produced inventive play, and was capable of commanding the respect of players and managers. Nothing that has happened in the two years since he came to us has reversed that opinion. In fact the opposite is true, his work with us has confirmed that original opinion and even enhanced it.'

## Organization update

Glen Kirton is happy with the way things are going, and has to report only a couple of problems. One concerns the television rights. The television stations who do not have broadcasting rights to the tournament do not have the right to any access at all. This means that as well as being banned from entering the stadiums, which is fair enough, they cannot even enter the team hotels or training grounds, which is ridiculous and doesn't help promote the tournament. Glen can see no reason why these excluded television stations should not have access to places outside the grounds such as the team bases.

The other problem is a dispute between official supplier BT, and official sponsor Mastercard. Mastercard have the exclusive rights to produce the official phonecard for the tournament, and they are objecting to BT's plans for account-holders to be able to use BT cards to access ordinary phones. BT have offered to put Mastercard's name on their phonecards. Anyway the BT cards aren't a full credit card and can only be used for the phones, but Mastercard have refused to allow BT to go ahead. This seems rather small-minded to me, and also costly. It could cost an extra two million pounds for BT to revise their system. This is a cost that will be borne by UEFA, as it is an unforeseen extra, but it seems pathetic that football should lose an extra two million pounds investment over something that should be sorted out fairly easily.

Now to tickets. Not surprisingly, several teams have requested an increase in their allocation of 7,000 tickets per match. The breakdown of ticket allocation is that approximately 50 per cent of tickets are sold on the English market. The rest are divided up. For example, ISL Marketing, the commercial rights sellers, will receive 3,000 tickets per match and 6,000 for the Final. The media take between 1,500 and 2,000, and then there are tickets for the hospitality packages and for the FA, UEFA and the European Broadcasting Union etc. By January 452,000 tickets for the public had been sold on the English market. The opening match, the

Final and the England v Scotland match were all sold out. Not a bad report four months before the tournament started.

Scotland have requested more tickets and will receive 8,000 for the England v Scotland match. Denmark and Turkey, who are playing in Nottingham and Sheffield, have requested more tickets for their matches and they will receive 10,000. Germany have requested more and will receive an extra allocation for their matches at Old Trafford. The Netherlands, like Scotland, will receive 8,000 rather than 7,000 for their match at Wembley against England, and between 9,500 and 10,000 for their matches at Villa Park.

Glen hasn't decided what he will do after the tournament. The FA has the option to talk to him first, but I have a feeling that after Euro 96 Glen will be off to work with UEFA in Switzerland, where he will be able to deploy his multi-faceted talents on an international stage.

It is always difficult to know how to finish a book that will be published before the event it is leading up to. I cannot look into a crystal ball and predict the outcome of the European Championship finals this summer. All I can promise is that I will be giving my all to ensure that the England team is well prepared and will give its best to recapture the glory of the past.

It is for this reason that I decided to hasten my decision on the renewal of my contract. It was impossible to go into a major tournament without having things settled; as I mentioned there would have been relentless press speculation as to whether I was going to continue or who was going to fill my shoes. Most other national football associations understand this and make their plans in advance. The Italian Football Federation has renewed the coach Arrigo Sacchi's contract for a further two years. He will be paid about £500,000 a year.

And what of my plans? For reasons known only to themselves, several newspapers linked me to the Arsenal manager's job, but there is no truth in that. In fact there is no truth in any report linking me to a club or national team.

After the European Championship Final, I am going to be a free agent, and concentrate on clearing my name in the various cases I am involved in. Then, and only then, will I decide on my football future. Being a positive character, I have this feeling that things will go well and you will see me back in football once more.

Through the pages of this book I have shared some of my thoughts and philosophy, and I have introduced you to the people who work with me, from the FA to my private office. I hope there will be a sequel, and that we can continue to follow their fortunes through the European Championship finals and beyond.

I'd like to end the book with a quotation. The man who said it, in 1910, is none other than the great American President, Theodore Roosevelt. It sums up all my thoughts and feelings on life and people. I bow down to the great man.

'It is not the critic who counts; not the man who points out how the strong man stumbles, or where the doer of deeds could have done them better. The credit belongs to the man who is actually in the arena, whose face is marred by dust and sweat and blood, who strives valiantly; who errs and comes short again and again; because there is not effort without error and shortcomings; but who does actually strive to do the deed; who knows the great enthusiasm, the great devotion, who spends himself in a worthy cause; who at the best knows in the end the triumph of high achievement and who at the worst, if he fails, at least he fails while daring greatly. So that his place shall never be with those cold and timid souls who know neither victory nor defeat.'

# ACKNOWLEDGEMENTS

The writing of this book has of its nature been fast and furious. Many have helped, and my great thanks go to all my friends and colleagues (on and off the pitch) for helping Jane Nottage and me make the book as all-encompassing, informative and up-to-the-minute as possible; especially Michelle Rogers, Frances Hart, Ted Buxton, David Davies, John Browett, Trevor Phillips, Graham Kelly, Glen Kirton, John Crane, Carlos Alberto Parreira, Ian Preece, David Hewett, Beata Zaborowska, Yola Bungy, Alan Smith, Dave Butler, Eddie Ashby, my family and all at the Football Association.